M000049536

⋙ LE COOL CHANGED MY LIFE ⋘

A WEIRD AND WONDERFUL GUIDE TO BARCELONA

Barcelona

2006–2007

First published in Great Britain in 2006 by Friday Books
An imprint of The Friday Project Limited
83 Victoria Street, London SW1H 0HW

www.thefridayproject.co.uk
www.fridaybooks.co.uk

© le cool publishing, s.l. 2006
www.lecool.com

The right of le cool to be identified as author/editor of this collection has been asserted
by it in accordance with the Copyright, Designs and Patents Act 1988.
Changing your life, one city at a time.

ISBN 1-905548-22-2
978-1-905548-22-4

British Library Cataloguing in Publication Data

A catalogue record for this book is available from the British Library

Design by Feriche Black

Produced by Staziker Jones and printed in Italy

It is the publisher's policy to use paper manufactured from sustainable forests.

Do you hear that? It's the pumping bass of a week-long *fiesta*. It's the rattle of a silver cocktail shaker. The chirrip of a bar filled with tiny caged birds, the heartbeat of a group playing bongos in the park, the yell of a seller of butane gas, the hush of the sea on the beach at midnight, the silence of midday in a hidden library.

Can you smell that? It's dope, it's fireworks, incense waved by a dancing transexual, it's olive oil cracking as it hits fresh lobster, it's sweat, it's perfume, it's freshly ground espresso, it's the aerosol tang of freshly sprayed graffiti.

Do you feel that? It rumbles underneath your feet. It's probably the Metro— or maybe it's the groan of the city itself, restless, throbbing. Moving.

Barcelona is not about weird old buildings or people standing still, painted blue. Neither is it sangria and naff discos filled with tourists, although thousands of people leave each year thinking it is. Barcelona is about being in the right place at the right time. It's about knowing the right bell to ring, the right drink to order, the right person to talk to. It's about being here, right now.

We've talked to all our friends, then invited their friends, their friends' friends, and then just dragged people in off the street to share their secrets in return for free beer. Some of these places have never appeared in guidebooks before; those that did have never been talked about properly. We've made it our mission to find the best that Barcelona has to offer.

You never get the best out of a place if you don't have a friend who can show you around. But where could you find one of those?

contents

ALSO...

WHAT YOU WON'T FIND

is how to get from the airport or where Las Ramblas is. If you want to send a postcard or know how much it costs to enter Sagrada Familia, this is not the book for you. Go back to the shelves and buy something else. There's plenty to choose from.

if you like what we're doing and want to see something amazing, turn to a page, any page, and the adventure starts here.

welcome to **le COOL** BARCELONA

Sleeping

Like any place filled with tourists, the city has accommodation for all ages, budgets and sexual preferences. The usual selection of hostels, hotels and luxury apartments is available. If you speak a bit of Spanish and want something more personal, a pension like Residencia Victoria (c/Comtal, 9, 1st floor 1st flat; Map 3 B2, cheapest room €24; Tel: 933 180 760; victoria@atriumhotels.com) is the place to head. It's friendly, has a sunny terrace and it's just as cheap as sharing a room full of Aussie backpackers.

For a space of your own and a proper kitchen, ApartHotels are the new big thing, apartments for rent with a cleaning service and often a concierge. Hispanos Siete Suiza (c/Sicilia, 255; from €185; Tel: 932 082 051; Metro: Sagrada Familia; www.barcelona19apart ments.com) is highly spoken of, as is the literary-themed Casa de Les Lletres (Plaça Antonio López, 6; from €180; Tel: 932 263 730; www.cru2001.com, Map 3 E2/3). **But hey, worst comes to it, just stay out really, really late. With clubs open all weekend, who needs a bed?**

this is AL and he runs a hostel

Al runs AlBerGuest, the friendliest backpacker hostel in town. It's also one of the cheapest (about €20 a night). Plus it's right next to Plaça Catalunya, it has a kitchen, free internet and all residents get a front door key, so there's no curfew. Some people love it so much, they stay for months at a time. But there's one catch: Al has to find you first. The hostel has no sign; you can't normally phone for a booking. To keep the place safe, Al himself chooses all the people who stay there rather than attract the passing trade. He goes to the bus stops and the train stations, and picks out the recent arrivals who are the kind of people he wants have around. Maybe you're one of them.

Phone Al on 635669021 or email alvand@alberguest.com and explain why you're the kind of person he wants to have around. Metro: Catalunya. Map 3 A2.

EXTRA! Al has a new luxury creative hostel for people who want to make things. Contact him and explain what you do. It might just change your whole Barcelona experience.

NAME Barcelona Center House
ADDRESS c/Comtal 9, principal 2ª
         Gotico (a couple of
         blocks from Plaza
         Catalunya)
PHONE 933 171 044
         www.barcelonacenter-house.com
PRICE Double 60-80€
       Triple 75-95€

Why stay in a hotel cubicle, when
you can have your own kitchen/
bedroom/bathroom combo with a
private terrace for the same price?

NAME Gothic Point
ADDRESS c/Vigatans 5, Metro Jaume I
Open all year, 24 hours a day
PHONE 932 687 808
www.gothicpoint.com

Colourful (thank Barcelona's
graffiti artists), artistic (thank
the owner strange tastes),
chilled (thank the large Terrace),
fun (thank heavens).
Perhaps the most sociable
youth hostel in the city.

As if dragged back from obscurity by a hip young filmmaker, this old-style hotel has been totally reinvented in the last two years. Its former draughty, old-style rooms are now modern-boutique stylish, and it's only the prices that remain B-movie cheap.

HOSTAL GOYA

Pau Claris, 74 1ª Map 5 C4
Prices around €70
Metro: Urquinaona
93 302 25 65
www.hostalgoya.com

HOTEL Banys Orientals

An elegant night's sleep for a great price in the trendy part of town. If you're planning on heading to bed early, rooms at the back are quieter.

Price: around €90 for a double room
c/Argenteria, 37 Map 2 B2
Tel: 93 268 84 60
Metro: Jaume I
www.hotelbanysorientals.com

OMM

As slick and smart as a white Prada suit, this is the largest arm of the mini local empire of the Tragaluz Group. Design is the priority at the Omm so expect acres of white space and, if you step into its lobby bar or basement club, people will check out how much your clothes match the décor. The place to stay for the young urban traveller who has the complete back issues of *Wallpaper**.

Hotel Omm c/Roselló, 265 Map 5 B4; From €230
Tel: 934 454 000; Metro: Diagonal; www.hotelomm.es

this is one of the best-located hotels in Europe. Hidden away in the Barrio Gothic and built inside an 18th-century palace, it's stylish and in the heart of the city, yet hidden away from all but those who know. When you walk in, it feels like a shrine to elegance. Everything the place does is as smooth and smart as black marble. If you can't stay there, you can still slide into the bar one night and, if you're subtle about it, enter during the day to sit on the sofas in their small library and read the day's American and British newspapers (first left as you enter). Before you know it, you're on the phone to your credit card company, explaining to them just how special a night there must be

Hotel Neri

c/Sant Sever, 5
Map 3 C2
€250 per night
Tel: 933 040 655
Metro: Jaume I
www.hotelneri.com

Hotel La Florida

If you're in the centre of town, look up. Find the fairytale church of Tibidabo and then move your gaze a little to the right, to a large squat building with its own watchtowers. This is Gran Hotel La Florida, the most luxurious in-the-city, out-of-the-city place for the night. You could create your own decadent soap opera in its grounds. There's a luxuriantly expansive terrace (perfect for a sip of cava, even if you're not staying there), plus exclusive club nights and a five-star elegance for those who quite literally like to look down on everyone else.

Crta Vallvidrera 83-93
€400 per night. Tel: 932 593 000.
Metro: you could take the funicular to Tibidabo and walk...
but if you're staying there, you'll probably take a cab.
Or have your own chauffeur.
www.hotellaflorida.com

A flat for rent with space for 18.

NONICO

Tel: **933 191 661**
Metro: Arc de Triomf
From €45 per person
www.decimononico.com

5 ROOMS

Yessica wants to invite you round to her place. Five rooms, comfy common areas, stylish artwork and a great way to avoid those hotel blues.

c/Pau Claris 72, 1
Map 5 C4
Metro: Catalunya
Tel: 933 427 880
€125 per double
www.thefiverooms.com

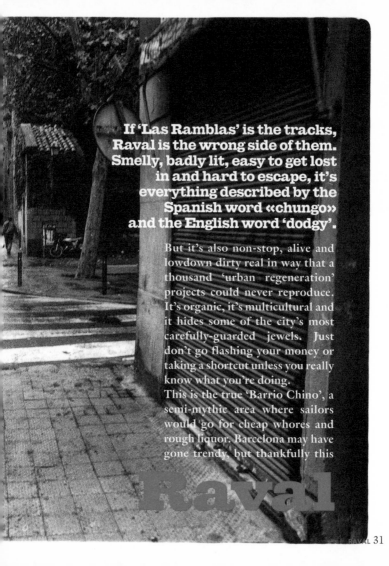

If 'Las Ramblas' is the tracks, Raval is the wrong side of them. Smelly, badly lit, easy to get lost in and hard to escape, it's everything described by the Spanish word «chungo» and the English word 'dodgy'.

But it's also non-stop, alive and lowdown dirty real in way that a thousand 'urban regeneration' projects could never reproduce. It's organic, it's multicultural and it hides some of the city's most carefully-guarded jewels. Just don't go flashing your money or taking a shortcut unless you really know what you're doing.

This is the true 'Barrio Chino', a semi-mythic area where sailors would go for cheap whores and rough liquor. Barcelona may have gone trendy, but thankfully this

Raval

part has kept its unique charm. It's also an area of high immigration, with an abundance of cheap curries and a lot of people doing little more than standing around, watching you go by. Two huge holes have been blasted out of the tight medieval mess of buildings. One is occupied by a weird art museum called the MACBA, and its Siamese twin, the only-slightly-more-conventional CCCB. On the other side of an empty square sits FAD, design-industry body with a trendy bar-restaurant (map 4 B2).

It houses tastes and smells you won't find anywhere else

Further south is Rambla del Raval, a recently cleared stretch of open ground where they flattened an entire housing block. Kebab shops face each other in a pita-filled stand-off, while some surprisingly good bars look on nervously in the corners. A fat metal cat by Botero grins, oblivious, in the centre. Raval is safe during the day and mostly ok at night. It houses late-night bars, clubs, tastes and smells you won't find anywhere else. There's gold and dragons in equal measure and it rewards those willing to take the adventure. We're just hoping that the 5* hotel under construction won't be the excuse the city council needs to sanitise the district of its fun.

THIS IS NOT A NORMAL CITY.

While all cities hide a certain level of weirdness beneath their roofs, when Barcelona lets go, it's like the whole place is one very wrong dream.

For instance, the people. As fixed as a shop or bar, certain characters are worthy of a guidebook of their own. The metro guy's one – he usually stands by the green line going north at Passeig de Gracia around 8-9am. His grey hair is smoothed back, his tie hangs off at an angle, he waves a baton, he stares wildly and he loudly sings opera at the passing commuters.

The Vagabondo del Verso, meanwhile, is a more sober character, a literary Argentine who lives on the streets and sells his poetry books from a moveable stall on Las Ramblas.

This is a city of strange.

On Friday nights at swish cocktail bar Dry Martini (see Drinking), the pseudo-glamorous Violeta La Burra often sells roses to the customers. La Burra is a drag queen in her declining years, but in the 1940s she was the darling of Dalí and the Parisian cabarets (these days, however, she's been spotted in the occasional porn film to make ends meet).

Perhaps her successor is the fellow seen mainly at the hippest parties and walking around Raval, who wears a long flowing dress and an Amish-style hat.

But the people are just the beginning. When you start to find what happens behind closed doors around here... let's just say that a little knowledge can be a scary thing. This is a city of strange. Turn on, go in, be freaked out.

They may be the only reason you'd come to this hole-in-the-wall, but the 60 or so birdcages on one side of this smoky, Old Spain establishment aren't the first thing you see upon entering. No, that would be the grizzled and entirely male clientele, chatting merrily away in Catalan through the thick smoke that has these caged birds singing like canaries in a coal mine. You can guess the age of this place by the mix of yellowed Spanish signs on the walls (*Members playing cards or dominoes cannot keep their birds on the table*, for one) while Catalan bulletins advertise competitions that take place in the back patio on Saturdays. Though Spanish signs say the coffee machine is only for members, sidle up to the counter and after the barkeep has finished with the cluster of songbird fans, he'll ask what you're having.

LA PRI MI TIVA

La Primitiva – Sant Martí
(Societat Ocellaire)
c/Meridiana, 157
Metro: Clot

If you want to escape the tourists, you won't find many down here. Five minutes off the Rambla and it's grim, scary and filled with some of the most unappealing hookers you'll ever see. Have a drink in one of the bars but don't sit on the sofas. You never know who'll be sitting next to you and rubbing your leg. When the five star hotel fills the gap at the end of the street it'll probably disappear, but for now there's nowhere quite like calle **Robadors**.

St Christopher is the patron saint of lightening, bookbinders and taxi drivers. But it's mainly just the TAXISTAS who visit the tiny, hidden 500·year-old San Cristobal del Regomir CHAPEL to receive a blessing.

No Fumar

THE SAINT'S HOLIDAY IS 10 JULY

C/REGOMIR 5, METRO JAUME I

OPEN FOR MASS ON SATURDAYS AT 7.30PM

la cuna de oro

If you're passing Jaume I metro on Via Laietana, turn into a small street and have a look at the shop of this aged Tarot card reader. It's a museum to fetishistic clutter, gifts from visitors from around the world.

c/Boria, 7
Metro: Jaume I
MAP 2 - A2

NO PERMITAS

Frederic Mares was probably
an obsessive compulsive. He
was likes geeky Citizen Kane
— he collected a thousand
objects from all over the
world, and then put them in
display cases. And what
objects they are. The nation's
finest collection of rusty iron
keys. The most complete set
of life-size 16th-century
crucifixes nailed to a wall.
The labels of a thousand
antique cigars. And, hidden
away behind a display board
in one of the smallest rooms,
a collection of Victorian
erotic cigarette cards. See the
coquettish maid strip for her
bath. Witness the mistress
getting ready for her bed.
Marvel at a collector who
knew exactly what he liked.
SECOND FLOOR ONLY OPEN

TUESDAY,THURSDAY, SATURDAY,
ROOM 58: TURN LEFT AS YOU
ENTER AND LOOK AT THE FRAMED
CARDS ON THE WALL TUCKED
BEHIND THE HINGED WOODEN
DISPLAY STANDS.

Museu
Frederic Mares

Plaça St Iu 5-6
Metro: Liceu/Jaume I
Map 3 Q2

The Kiss of Death.

In a quiet corner in Departmento
Tercero in the Cemetario Viejo
(aka Cementeri de l'est), Poble
Nou. Near Bogatell beach.

Enter via Avenida Icaria.
Metro: Llacuna

Museum of Funeral Carriages

There's no sign to suggest it, but buried beneath the local government's funeral services office in a district filled with undertakers is the creepy Museum of Funeral Carriages. If you ask nicely at the front desk, they'll call a security guard to turn on the lights and show you around. In a slow march, naturally.

c/Sancho de Avila, 2
Metro: Marina
Monday-Friday 10am-1pm, 4-6pm

The bar **Casa Paco** (c/Allada de Vermell,10; Metro: Arc de Triomf) is the centre of the universe for me. All my friends are here and I've had some good nights. Sometimes I even help pick up the glasses and clear the tables away. They closed it for a week once and I nearly went crazy. If we want to go clubbing after, we'll go the **Sala Apolo** (c/Nou de la Rambla 113; Metro: Paral.lel).

My favourite place for breakfast is **Casa Casals** in Plaça Victor Balaguer (Metro: Jaume I). They only run it in the morning, and they do very good ciabattas with bacon and cheese. It's very Catalan. Simple, cheap, high quality and you can sit outside.

For dinner, my favourite at the moment is **Made in Italy** (c/Ample, Metro: Jaume I). And then with few mates, I do a fish club in **La Panadeta** (c/Comercial, 7; Metro: Arc de Triomf). Once a month we go there and stuff ourselves with seafood.

When I want to buy records, for non-DJ stuff I go to c/Tallers (Metro: Plaça Catalunya) and visit **CD Drome** for its independent selection. And **Disco Castelló** – two shops side-by-side where you can find all sorts of stuff. They have some great selections in the corners – some old rock 'n' roll and rockabilly.

For DJ stuff, it's **Tazmania** or **Wah-wah** (see Shopping chapter). They play a lot of house here in Barcelona, but underneath, this is a techno city.

CRISTIAN VOGEL
IS AN INTERNATIONAL TECHNO **DJ** FROM THE UK. HE'S BEEN LIVING IN BARCELONA FOR MORE THAN FIVE YEARS.

SOME THOUGHTS ABOUT THE CATALANS

BARCELONA

le cool press

2006

They speak a strange language. They work ostentatiously hard. And they rule Barcelona. If you want to get the most out of your time here, you've got to learn how to tell the locals apart from their Spanish counterparts. As any proud Catalan will tell you, This Is Not Spain.

The former kingdom of Catalonia was never about bullfights and flamenco. Instead, it has its own, seemingly contradictory traditions: while the people have a markedly reserved sociability (house parties are rare), there is also a Mediterranean zest for life (celebrations include placing children at the top of freestanding, multi-storey human castles on 11 September, or dancing near papier-mâché dragons spewing very real fireworks on the festival of Mercè at the end of September).

These people are survivors, partly thanks to their economic savvy. The industrial revolution arrived in Catalonia before the rest of the Iberian peninsula, following Barcelona's brief trade empire across the Mediterranean. With its fertile green spaces, this autonomous region has always been an enormous agricultural boon to the Spanish state. When the Catalans complain about their tax profits flowing out of Catalonia, the rest of Spain calls them money-grabbing and miserly – whereas here they say they've worked hard and deserve to see their money spent in their own territory, rather than doled out to the usual suspects in Andalucía and Murcia. The city has already received its own present from these regions courtesy of Franco, who moved people from the south up to Barcelona, in order to dilute the city's Catalanity.

Residents of Catalonia are much more likely to travel and learn foreign languages than in Castile or Aragon, and when it comes to tolerating political dissidents, the further to the left the better. Although Catalan high-society is very conservative, they still show a bemused tolerance for self-imposed social exiles. And so Barcelona and its surrounding countryside have become a squatters' mecca, bringing in idealistic young anarchists and the usual anti-capitalist contingents. This may stem from a natural Catalan sympathy for the stateless minority, itself an established culture that's all-too-often overshadowed by an imperialist neighbour. Of course, the standard explanations for squats in abandoned buildings apply here too – slow response times from city bureaucracy, lax enforcement of too many laws to list – but the sheer number of *okupas*, coupled with Barcelona's reputation as the youth capital of Europe, may also point to a different conclusion.

The Catalans are so used to being underdogs that their national day – 11 September – commemorates a defeat in 1714. The most recent Catalan attempt for independence was in 1931, but the republic lasted only a few years before it was crushed by Franco. Most bureaucrats with seniority today have stories of civil disobedience during the dictator's regime. Even the older generation with respectable jobs in finance often hold a soft spot in their hearts for unbridled activism, and many are happy to re-adjust their glasses and look the other way. But they'd likely never admit to doing so; that reserved personality makes sure that these soft spots are well-hidden.

Barcelona's Catalans can be difficult to get to know, although throwing out a few phrases in their language can help break through the all-business exteriors. Even establishing casual friendships with Catalans can be tough: but once they've established a relationship, their loyalties run deep and passionate, so they are naturally cautious when meeting new people. Often your quirky Catalan acquaintances will be happy to take you out for drinks, but would be horrified if you asked to come up for coffee. Home dinner parties and casual hanging out are reserved for close friends. The Catalan social group, known as the *colla*, is formed early on, usually in childhood, and for many Catalans, the members of their *colla* will be the ones they spend their evenings with for the rest of their lives.

More than anything else, Catalans are careful. They've been burned by enough failed alliances and cultural cleansing initiatives (the language has been banned several times, including throughout the 40-year dictatorship) to prepare first and play later. They build everything – businesses, relationships, human castles – from the ground up, with a studied and steady hand. And they believe they should be able to enjoy the payoff: it's been more than seventy years since they were this close to a republic, with Catalan street signs on every corner and traditional dances in front of the Catedral on Sundays. Citizens of the "Catalan Country", as it's known in both of its official languages, have every reason to be proud of what they have recreated. And every reason to keep striving for more.

═══ *Spotter's guide:* ═══

• The best place to spot a Catalan – or 99,000 of them – is Camp Nou, the FC Barcelona stadium.

• Groups of young Catalans hang out in Plaça del Sol (Metro: Fontana); wouldbe revolutionaries go on Saturday nights.

• On Sundays, the family heads to a bar and have vermouth and cockles in a spicy sauce, eg. Bar Ciurana (c/Vallespir, corner Can Bruixa; Metro: Les Corts), before buying a cake at a bakery like Foix (Plaça de Sarría).

• Famed okupa communes include Can Mas Deu (Antic Camí de Sant Llàtzer; www.canmasdeu.net; Metro: Canyelles) and one right by the bottom corner of Parc Güell.

sh

Kerching.
Swipe.
Click.
Wallets at
forty paces.
Cover me,
I'm going in.

shoppi

Quirky clothing

could be the slogan for **c/Avinyó** (Metro: Jaume I) and the streets surrounding it. We could choose any shops at random to recommend – such as the funky **Tribu** at no.12 with a great chic shoe selection in the back room – but walk around and check everything out. Just off Avinyó is the infamous Plaça Trippy (**Plaça George Orwell**), the perfect place to accessorise.

c/Porta ferrisa

In a similar vein, just off La Rambla there are a few such stores. A solitary camel marks the entrance to a piecemeal collection of unusual clothes, jewellery and a

ng

a solitary camel marks the entrance

hidden cafe at the back in which to contemplate your purchases. Also on Portaferissa is **Mayday**, a clothing store filled with next year's must-have brands. **c/Petritxol**, down a nearby sidestreet, has a couple of unusual clubwear shops if that's your thing. The short but busy **c/Pelayo,** stretching from Plaça Catalunya to Plaça Universitat, has the highest concentration of shoe stores and is the place to make your feet as hip as your body. And if you're hunting for collective individuality, head to **Passeig del Born** and the little streets around it, but be warned that creativity doesn't come cheap.

If Donna Karan, Armani and their superchic superpriced friends are your bread and butter, get a cab up to **Via Augusta** on the corner of **Travessera de Gracia**. A stroll down towards **Diagonal** from there offers a range of **high-class shops.**

Back in the centre, **Passeig de Gracia** is Barcelona's Champs Elysée. Keep your eyes open for **Boulevard Rosa** at Passeig de Gracia, 55, an upmarket shopping centre hidden inside a modernist block.

ng

But shopping's not just about the new and the latest to impress label-watchers and upmarket wine bars. Other things you should know about:

second hand tat (with the occasional lump of gold) is at Mercat Encants in Plaça de la Glòries (Metro: Glòries), which contains most things, from old porn to bedsprings. All the streets around are lined with similar. Make sure you go in the morning and root around into every nook and cranny.

wine Vinoteca on c/Agullers (Metro: Jaume I) isn't cheap but it's probably the most comprehensive wine shop in the city; it certainly has the most knowledgeable staff.

If its CD **electronics** players, cameras, consoles or mobile phones you're after, a walk down c/Reina Cristina (Metro: Barceloneta) usually covers it.

There's a **computer** wide selection of mostly **equipment** low-budget shops on both sides of Ronda St Antoni, starting at Plaza Universitat. (Metro: Universitat).

We're not sure **flowers** why you'd need **24 hours** it, but you never **a day** know when you might have a row with your partner or meet a pretty girl at 4am. Luckily for you, the flower sellers on c/Valencia between c/Roger de Lluria and c/Bruc never close.

SHOPPING

When you head towards the hills, the streets get wider and the shop space bigger. Tucked between uptown snob and downtown quirky is Eixample, a grid of streets tarmacked with style. On the left is Gayxample, full of hip and stylish menswear. In the centre, women can find the names they need to complete their label collection. It may be hard on the feet (nb. good excuse to buy shoes), but these streets are paved with pure golden clothes hangers. Retail therapy so effective, they should offer it on prescription.

M69 It feels strange asking the shop assistant to bring you a size 14 year old because you've burst the seams of the size 12 year old. But as any gay man will know, French childrenswear-maker Petit Bateau makes the best tank tops and not an eyelid is batted, not even when you ask to try a pair of Bikkemberg leather pants Essentials for the modern gay man. **MUNTANER 69**

NORMAN VILATA

One of a rare breed of hand-made shoe artisans, Norman styles, hammers and carves the leather himself to suit the needs of each customer's left and right plates of meat.

ENRIC GRANADOS 5, MAP 5 C3

JUAN ANTONIO LÓPEZ

A spacious boutique with a minimalist décor – but then it's all about the floors in a women's shoe shop. Novel designs and materials are used in a range of summer colours by this famed local designer. The style is elegant and poised, while hinting at hidden thrills.

CONSELL DE CENT 240, MAP 5 C3

LA BOUTIQUE DEL HOTEL

A small shrine to men's high fashion inside Hotel Axel. Worshippers of John Richmond, Helmut Lang and the like will be able to find their own souvenirs of Barcelona here.

ARIBAU 33, MAP 5 B2/3

EDUARD BOLDOVA

Be you boy or girl, you slink in wearing a hat and dark glasses. And you leave loud and proud, with a beauty treatment, great hairdo and new t-shirt to change your identity and give your self-confidence a huge headstart.

CASANOVA 72, MAP 5 C3

TONI MIRO

Be calm as you glide through this classic Catalan store, its famed men's collection and newly-added women's range in the relaxed style of the shop. The cut is as sharp as a silver scalpel, the materials and colours as fine as you would expect. As are the prices.

CONSELL DE CENT 349-351, MAP 5 C4

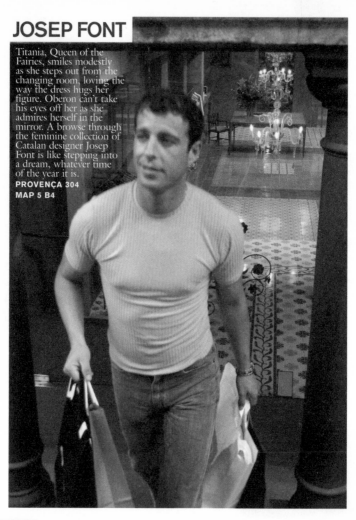

JOSEP FONT

Titania, Queen of the Fairies, smiles modestly as she steps out from the changing room, loving the way the dress hugs her figure. Oberon can't take his eyes off her as she admires herself in the mirror. A browse through the feminine collection of Catalan designer Josep Font is like stepping into a dream, whatever time of the year it is.

PROVENÇA 304
MAP 5 B4

JEAN PIERRE BUA

There is life after Armani. Just ask the snob, the eccentric, the bohemian, the mother and the daughter, the husband, the lover, the homo, the hetero, the metro. The exuberance of Mami, the shapes of Gaultier, Balenciaga reinvented by Nicolas Ghesquière… the home of Catalan flair is Jean Pierre Bua. Give yourself up to him and let him cover you in his particular style. Trust him, he's a professional.

DIAGONAL 469, MAP 5 A2

NOTENOM

They didn't heed the warning. Don't cross the streams, as the saying goes. But by throwing in Cacharel and Maurizio Pecoraro next to local boys Locking Schocking or David Delfin, you can't help but admire the keymaster's selection.

PAU CLARIS 159, MAP 5 B4

2 RAS

Design junkies take note: this little bookshop/gallery run by local publisher Actar is filled with all the design porn you and your black-polonecked, Apple computer-filled, bare floorboard studio needs. Also check out the gallery space at the back.

Doctor Dou 10

1 SPIKE

Very masculine casualwear for those who take their image seriously. With a large selection of clothes from a range of labels, its popularity doesn't hinder the ever-attentive service.

Hospital 46

Plaça
Urquinaona

RAVAL WALK

4 U-CASAS

Casual and sporty footwear with an eye for the special. The shoes are practical, comfortable and include some of the most coveted names in trainer-wear. Comfort was never so cool.

Tallers 2

5 CASAS INTER NACIONAL

Put creativity onto your feet. Man or woman, Italian or Spanish, the quality, materials and exclusive designs will turn heads at the ball.

Rbla Canaletes 125

Pg Picasso

3 NAIFA

A shop filled with self-designed womenswear that flaunts in all areas everything that is true Barcelonawear: casual, unique and always chic.

Doctor Dou 11

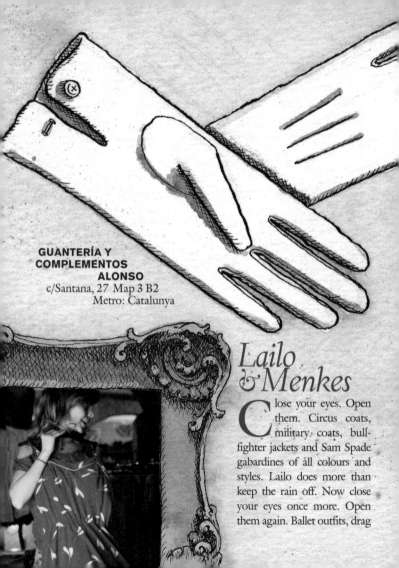

Lailo
&Menkes

Close your eyes. Open them. Circus coats, military coats, bullfighter jackets and Sam Spade gabardines of all colours and styles. Lailo does more than keep the rain off. Now close your eyes once more. Open them again. Ballet outfits, drag

gloves & hats

The Alonso glove shop and the Obach hat shop. Two steps back into an earlier time, when craftsmanship and personal service were what a gentleman or lady would expect. For admirers of the gloves of Gilda or the hat of Ava Gardner in Mogambo, this is the style of a bygone age which never truly went out of fashion.

SOMBRERERIA OBACH
c/Call, 2.
Metro: Liceu. MAP 3 C2

queen shoes, wild clothes from all ages, styles and exuberance. Imagination made out of fabric. Menkes is playing dress-up, grown-up style. These shops are a magical mystery tour-de-force. Don't stress, just play.

LAILO: c/ Riera Baixa, 20. Map 4 C3. Metro: Universitat.

MENKES: Gran Vía de les Corts Catalanes, 646. Map 5 C4. Metro: Urquinaona.

7 FARM4

Hard to find but worth the effort, Farm4 houses exclusive labels and limited edition clothes, all courtesy of a local collective. Spacious and relaxing, the shop is lined with sixties décor and has a chill-out space at the back.

Baixada de Viladecols 3

2 PLAÇA VILA DE MADRID

Doggy Bag, in the plaça's corner, is great for bags and complements. A passage called Galeries Citadines leads to Las Ramblas with Erreté, a funky selection of secondhand clothes, and then Evelyn & T.N.T is as kitschy and crazy as it gets.

GOTHIC WALK

5 KOPP

Funny knick-knacks, gratuitous tat and kitsch kitchenware, Kopp is stocked from bottom to top with plastics, patterns, prints and paraphernalia. Wedged with widgets, gorged with gizmos, this is the place to pick up the perfect present.

Avinyó 37

3 SO_DA

When it's all getting a bit much, slide into this minimalist boutique and head to the bar at the back. When you emerge from a swift pick-you-up, the clothes will have a similar effect. Most items are exclusive to the shop, the rest imported from Parisian showrooms.

Avinyó 24

Parallel

4 ZSU ZSA

Most of the lines are designed by the owners María and Mónica, but it's also a launch-pad for Spain's new designers of the moment. The clothes are for young but smarter women, and lean towards the feminine. For a touch of luxury, they also offer made-to-measure.

Avinyó 50

1 MERCÈ MUNNÈ

A small boutique filled with the owner's own jewellery designs, plus womenswear designed by her daughter and other friends. The wedding dresses are worth a look even if you're not about to tie the knot.
Amargòs 18

6 PAPA BUBBLE

As tempting to your eyes as it is to your tongue. Surrounded by bags of coloured sweets and huge stripy lollipops, in Papabubble you can watch while the craftsmen roll out and shape homemade confectionery into hundreds of mouth-watering pieces of delight. If you smile sweetly, you might even get a free sample.
Ample 28

When I shop for more designer things I head to **Jean Pierre Bua** (see p57) to talk to Luis – he has great taste and is always very sensitive for what you're looking for. And then I go to **So_da** in c/Avinyó, 24 (Metro: Liceu), which I like a lot, especially for special items. For second-hand stuff I go to **c/Riera Baixa** (Metro: Liceu) – that entire part of Raval has lots of interesting odd clothing stores.

Being a super trainer fan, I shop at **Free** on c/Bonsuccés or the one next door at Placa de Vincenç Martorell. Sometimes I go to **Kwatra**, an "unofficial" Nike store in c/Antic de San Juan (Metro: Jaume I) and a real favourite, the **New Concept Store** on c/Duc de la Victoria. (Metro: Liceu).

If you want a tailored suit, of course there's **Bel** on Psg de Gracia, who's very classical. But there's an Argentine shirt tailor called **Raul Gonzalez** I went to once who was also very good. His atelier is at the junction of c/Casanova with Diagonal (Metro: Diagonal). He helped me once sew a couple of long neck shirts in pure Mafia style.

One up-and-coming designer worth watching: **Cecilia Sorensen**. She has an interesting visual language and her own store Comité on c/Notariat (Metro: Catalunya), specialising in women's clothes.

CHU UROZ
IS THE PRESIDENT OF INFLUENTIAL
MODAFAD
(AN ASSOCIATION FOR FASHION DESIGNERS) AND AT EVERY PARTY IN THE CITY.

3 LOISAIDA

A warehouse that could hold all-nighters houses a boutique selling vintage renewals, treasures from the Far East, and name brands such as Nolita and Indian Rose.

Flassaders, 42

BORN WALK

4 KWATRA

All work and no play... or maybe it's the other way around. Kwatra isn't just a sports shop, but instead mixes athletic wear with more casual outfits. Limited edition Nikes sit alongside Diesel and Quiksilver.

Antic de St Joan 1

1 OSCAR H GRAND

This smart tailors offers made-to-measure for men who like to look smart, modern yet with a touch of the classic, all with a high-quality cut. The shop shows Oscar's collection in segments, with new temptations on show in every visit.

Barra de Ferro 7

2 LA COMERCIAL MAN / WOMAN

Isabel Marant, Paul&Joe, Comme des Garçons, Cacharel, Amaya Arzuaga, Jocomomola, Paul Smith... and in anything but a cold megastore. A smart selection of certain brands from a local point of view. Don't miss the shoes from Juan Antonio López.

Rec 52 / 73

5 AGUA DEL CARMEN

If you're bored of the latest hip whatever (is that a shirt or a pair of trousers?), this tiny shop with a high ceiling has simple tastes and stylish colours.

Bonaire 5

OUTLETS

Big names don't always mean big prices. This is where label lovers in the know gather to fill their wardrobes.

LE SHOE
Shoes from top designers like Marc Jacobs, Sonia Rykiel, and Carachel in a modest setting with equally modest prices.
C/ VALENCIA 256 (ON THE CORNER OF RAMBLA CATALUNYA). MAP 5 B4.
METRO: PASSEIG DE GRACIA.

LOGO
Denim from names such as D&G, Fornarina, and Miss Sixty, for around 60 euros a pair.
C/ CANUDA, 15. MAP 3 B2.
METRO: PLAÇA CATALUNYA

OUTLET DEL BORN
Men's and women's apparel from Versace, Armani, Paul Smith and more.
C/ ESPARTERÍA, 12. MAP 2 C4. METRO: JAUME I

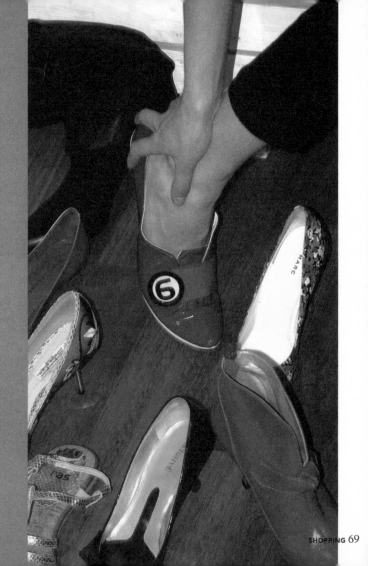

MÓN DE MONES

As soon as you enter, you're a child again, wanting to touch everything. The walls are dripping with shiny metals and coloured beads from the accessories mostly made in the workshop at the back. There is also a shiny selection of clothes, and all at pocket-money prices.

XIQUETS DE VALLS 9
MAP 6 C2

PLAZA DEL SOL

(CENTRE OF THE GRACIA SOLAR SYSTEM)

SUITE

With cutting-edge fashion and carefully-chosen colours, Suite is the snobbiest shop in the area. But that doesn't stop it from being fun, especially as they only fill their racks with work from up-and-coming local designers.

VERDI 3-5
MAP 6 B3

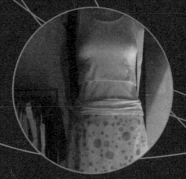

RED MARKET

The window display of Red Market entices red-faced fashion victims through its doors, to emerge red-hot and sizzling in the latest collection of international streetwear labels such as Gola, Aem Kei and DSL 55.

VERDI 20
MAP 6 B3

ELISA BRUNELLS

This is the home of exclusive silver and enamel jewellery, crafted in the tiny workshop overlooking the shop. Geometric designs with colours and images, the pieces are all one-offs and can be made to order. The shop also offers a treasure chest of scarves, shoes, bags and watches by other designers.

TORRENT DE L'OLLA 30
MAP 6 E2

CAMISERÍA PONS

It is what it was, and for many years to come. The classical Camiseria Pons shirt-maker has been in the city for more than 100 years and has moved on to selling other local designers without losing the particular Pons family style. Everything changes, everything stays the same.

GRAN DE GRÀCIA 49
MAP 6 D1

music

Wah Wah
Huge selection of just everything, from psychodelia through garage punk to 60s electronica. Excellent funk and soul section. c/Riera Baixa 14, Metro: Universitat, Map 4 B3.

CD Drome
Indie kid heaven. Loads of obscure pop and electronica and, despite the name, a decent selection of vinyl and obscure music DVDs too. c/Valldoncella 3, Metro: Universitat, Map 4 A4.

Daily Records
Ska, punk, soul, reggae and sixties. Run by one of the lynchpins of the city's mod scene, it stocks a great selection of hard-to-find British and Jamaican music. Good place to find out about gigs. c/Sitges 9 Metro: Catalunya, Map 4 B4.

Revolver
National and imported CDs from indie to techno on the ground floor, new and used vinyl upstairs. Decks available so you can try before you buy. c/Tallers 11, Metro: Catalunya, Map 4 B4.

Castelló
A quality new store with a tiny space for indie gigs at the back. Francesc Cambó 36, Metro: Jaume I.

Rimshot
Excellent reggae specialist. The best place in town to buy imported and classic Jamaican music. They'll even sell you a cold Red Stripe beer if you ask nicely. c/Gignas 9, Metro: Jaume I, Map 3 E2.

Sci Fi
New and classic electronic music to listen to and spin. c/Bonsuccés, Metro: Catalunya, Map 4 B4.

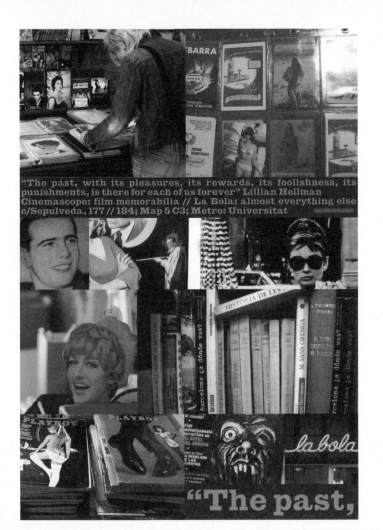

"The past, with its pleasures, its rewards, its foolishness, its punishments, is there for each of us forever" Lillian Hellman
Cinemascope: film memorabilia // La Bola: almost everything else
c/Sepulveda, 177 // 184; Map 5 C3; Metro: Universitat

"The past,

OLD SCHOOL RULES

If modern fashion makes you shriek, c/Riera Baixa in Raval (Map 4 B3) is your vintage saviour. Filled from top to tail with vintage boutiques, unique outfits spring from every clothes rail, be it a 60s dress, some worn-in cowboy boots or a sweater that your granddad would be proud of. **LE SWING** (number 13) is the place to pick up lavishly stylish vintage heels without the lavish price. **LAILO** (Riera Baixa, 20) and **HOLALA IBIZA** (Riera Baixa, 11) are also good for a retro fix.

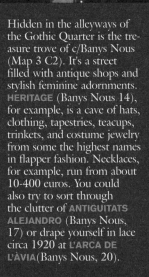

Hidden in the alleyways of the Gothic Quarter is the treasure trove of c/Banys Nous (Map 3 C2). It's a street filled with antique shops and stylish feminine adornments. **HERITAGE** (Banys Nous 14), for example, is a cave of hats, clothing, tapestries, teacups, trinkets, and costume jewelry from some the highest names in flapper fashion. Necklaces, for example, run from about 10-400 euros. You could also try to sort through the clutter of **ANTIGUITATS ALEJANDRO** (Banys Nous, 17) or drape yourself in lace circa 1920 at **L'ARCA DE L'ÀVIA** (Banys Nous, 20).

Modulolab: If retro furniture is your forward thrust, reach for your bakelite phone and book an appointment at the secret cave of Modulo Lab. Tel: 659 978 977; Metro: Universitat/Catalunya; www.modulolab.com

design

Vinçon: It's like your own sitting room in some of the most expensive real estate in Europe. Vinçon is a hyper-stylish design shop created in an incredible former flat on Passeig de Gracia, right by La Pedrera. Though the products themselves are impressive, the best way to enjoy this shop is to do what we do: go upstairs, find yourself a quiet room, sit on a sofa for a while and chill. Maybe you'd like to read a design book on its stunning terrace, or perhaps flick through a magazine on a chair overlooking the most expensive street in town. Every now and then you might like to glance out of the window and wave at the tourist buses. If they installed working TV sets, we'd never leave.
Passeig de Gracia, 98; Map 5 C4; Metro: Passeig de Gracia

l'appartement: Dress up your house as you'd dress your dream lover – with style, grace and a sense of humour. c/ Enric Granados, 44; Map 5 C3; Metro: Passeig de Gracia

Lobby: Never mind the function, feel the design. The Roca-Bonet family have put their passion for style into a shop called Lobby and they'll sell anything – books, clothes, tinned food, toothpaste – as long as the aesthetic is right. The father and son also design clothes that sit on the racks next to Issey Miyake and David Delfín. c/Ribera 5; Map 2 C5/6; Metro: Jaume I

Dom: Plastic fantastic, pop art and backlighting, psychodelia, memorabilia, dress up, get down and build your house in the manner to which Lenny Kravitz has become accustomed. c/Provença, 249-251; Metro: Diagonal, and c/Avinyó, 7; Metro: Liceu

they were the uncool kids in the playground

exchanging comic books and rolling weird-looking dice. But now they've grown up. Now they have money. And this is where they shop. Actually three shops all next to each other, Freaks is all that gives 'cult' a good name, selling everything from weird photography books to graphic novels, from examples of Tokyo graffiti to 1970s fighting manuels by Bruce Lee. Keep an eye out for the small stand in the comics section, filled with the best in Spanish fanzines. Now who's cool?

c/Ali Bei 10; Metro: Arc de Triomf

When the city walls finally fell in 1860 and Barcelona was allowed to expand, it decided to do so in octagonal Lego. The Sim City player of his day was ILDEFONS CERDÀ, who designed big blocks and wide avenues named Eixample (Eye-shamp-luh. It means 'extension').

The original plan was that each BLOCK would only have flats on two sides, the other two sides forming a park where all classes of people in neighbouring blocks would frolic together like one big hippy family.

The curly-moustachioed property developers soon put paid to that, however, and now only a handful of blocks maintain any idea of common space amid the buildings. Try c/Roger de Llúria, 58 for the hidden entrance to a small park, with its own water tower – and a paddling pool that becomes a mini "beach" in the summer.

THE PERFECT

MEASURING 113.3M ON EACH SIDE.

Living in the Eixample – as 262,000 people do – means long thin corridors, lots of small dark rooms that face internal corridors, and one glorious space with a balcony and lots of light. Some balconies face the road, while others the inside of the block, where everyone lives out their own version of REAR WINDOW. See how it looks by visiting DIY superstore Servei Estació, on c/Aragón 270-2. As you go upstairs, you have a great view of the inside of the block behind tourist favourite Casa Battló.

The Eixample HIDES EVERYTHING from 5* hotels to churches, night-clubs to car show-rooms, and all the local shops and restaurants you could need. Because of the form of the streets and the buildings, nothing is visible for more than half a block, which gives the Eixample a unique feeling, representing both hidden and visible in equal measure.

EIXAMPLE

there's always the big boys, of course. The **MACBA** (Plaça dels Àngels; www.macba.es) is probably the biggest, with the **CCCB** on its back wall (c/Montalegre, 5; Metro: Universitat; www.cccb.es) and local Tate Modern-esque gallery **CaixaForum** ten minutes away (Avda. Marqués de Comillas, 6-8; Metro: Espanya; www.caixaforum.es). Between the three of them, they cover most of the big-name famous worthies. But the city has a lot more refreshing offerings for those who can find them.

Coldcreation (c/Aragó, 379; Metro Tetuan; www.coldcreation.com), for instance, is an international contemporary gallery where new technologies are often mixed with interactive performances and installations. It also showcases 'porno-art', so leave Grandma at the hotel.

Metrònom (c/Fusina, 9; Metro: Jaume I) is another important space dedicated to new technology. It was known as a pioneer in the art world of the 80s and has remained cutting-edge. Just nearby there's the **Iguapop Gallery** (c/Comerç,15), whose exhibitions are usually connected to music, design and fashion. Up the road is the graffiti hangout **Montana** (c/Comerç, 6). And just across the road is the **Convento de Sant Agustí** (c/Comerç, 36), a 15th-century convent converted into a stunning space that's regularly used for performances and installations.

A short walk away in the Gothic quarter is **Maxalot** (c/Palma de Sant Just, 9; www.maxalot.com), a working design studio that frequently hosts exhibitions from commercial graphic designers – and has its own line in designer wallpaper.

Up on Montjuïc, the **Piscines Picornell** (Av. de l'Estadi 30-40; Metro: Espanya) aren't just the former set of one of Kylie Minogue's videos, as they regularly present art installations in the swimming pools, working alongside the **Massana Art School** to create one of the more unusual display spaces, and one with a stunning view of the city.

On the other side of the city, **Poblenou** is a popular artists' hangout filled with working studios. **Hangar** (Passatge del Marquès de Sta. Isabel, 40; Metro: Poblenou) sums up the feeling of the area nicely. It's a visual arts production centre, an artists' residence and a creative laboratory. There's also the fast-growing, hidden space/magazine **Espai Pupu** (c/Zamora 46-48, ático local 2; www.espaipupu.com).

The biggest trend at the moment is for video art; to see some of the best, try to catch the touring **RESFEST** festival in December.

If your culture is usually sampled via the silver screen, there's the **Barcelona Asian Film Festival** in May, the **Barcelona Jewish Film Festival** in July, the independent **La Alternativa** in November and, down the coast in neighbouring town **Sitges**, a major animation festival and one of Europe's bigger horror/sci-fi gatherings in October.

And for those who like their action in the flesh, indie theatre can be caught at **Mercat de les Flors** (c/Lleida, 59; Metro: Espanya), **L'Antic Teatre** (c/Verdaguer i Callis, 12; Metro: Urquinaona; www.lanticteatre.com), Teatre **Llantiol** (c/Riereta 7; Metro: St Antoni/Liceu) and **Artenbrut** (c/Perill, 9-10; Metro: Diagonal/Verdaguer).

culture

The new anti-graffiti rules are killing street art, the city is becoming grey. The other night I painted something and the next morning, when I went to take a photo of it, it had been cleaned away. These guys are going hardcore. The best places to do graffiti are now high up, because the street cleaners can't reach that far. I have a four-metre pole I take out with me to paint. If you want to paint, you should go out at 3 or 4am to avoid trouble, and go during the week when there are less people around. Remember that the **secret police** always go around in pairs, so if you see them coming while you are painting, just pretend to be talking on the phone.

I usually eat shawarma kebabs when I'm out. The best is on **Rambla del Raval,** there's a place at the top on the right-hand side where the walls are covered in a mosaic of tiny mirrors. As for bars, **Gusto** (Francisco Giner 24, Gracia) is one of the few places where I feel comfortable. You can smoke, the lighting is nice, there are pictures on the walls and they have good live music. Another cool bar is the **C3**, a bar at the CCCB museum.

My favourite smell is when I come across someone in the street **smoking a joint**. Even with the new laws, people seem to continue smoking in the street. I like that.

The first thing people have to see when they come to Barcelona is the sculpture of **Ariadna by Josep Maria Subirachs**. It's a 3D face carved into a wall (Passeig de Gracia 120, on the Sabadell bank), and as you move, it follows you with its gaze. It's incredible.

LOLO

IS AN ARGENTINIAN ARTIST WHO MOVED TO BARCELONA IN 2000. HE OFTEN DRAWS ON OBJECTS HE FINDS IN THE STREET. HE'S CURRENTLY WORKING ON A BOOK.

The noise, the traffic, the tourists, the everything

relax

The city rushes around

you

and all you want to do

is

e s c a p e

You need to leave it all behind

but you haven't got the time or the inclination to travel anywhere else.

These are the emergency exits hidden

in Barcelona's

streets

when all you want to do is close your eyes and r e l a x .

Just for a while, it's time to leave it all

behind.

UNIVERSITY
GARDENS

Everyone forgets about the University Gardens. At weekends, only the back door is open while the students are at home, rolling and smoking their lecture notes. Publicowned and open to all, hardly anyone remembers that its peaceful green corners are the perfect place to sit by a tree in the heart of the city and just let go.

WEEKDAYS: WALK THROUGH THE MAIN DOORS ON PLAÇA UNIVERSITAT, WEEKENDS: ENTER VIA C/DIPUTACIO METRO: UNIVERSITAT, MAP 5 C3

Sometimes all you want to do is spend the evening in a quiet corner with a good book. Lletraferit is filled with them, second-hand and in more than four languages. Order a beer/coffee/sandwich, curl up in one of the comfy chairs, stay late – and if you find yourself swallowed by the story you've picked up, buy it on your way out.

c/ Joaquín Costa 43; Map 4 B3
Metro: Universitat. Open until 2am during the week, 3am at weekends.

he
was SOO SWEET
— a thick
accent that stirred
me inside.

...WHERE IS HE?

WAS IT THIS TIME?
IS THE ANSWER SOME-
WHERE AT THE BOTTOM
OF THIS CUP?

→ STILL NO SIGN. BUT
THERE'S STILL SOME
chocolate LEFT...

He just called. I have the wrong
location. Who cares. In a happy
place. Time for more chocolate

ROMPEOLAS At the end of the beach: the sea wall.
The waves, the clouds, the occasional fisherman and just you.

obsolete grandeur
if the tracks are paved over
come in for the calm

trains glide out soundless
as you sit / on a stone bench
no pickpockets here

ESTACIÓ DE FRANÇA
Avinguda del Marquès de l'Argentera
Metro: Barceloneta

SSSH. SINGLE FILE, MOUTHS SHUT.

I'm going to tell you a secret but you can't say a word. This is the most peaceful corner of the city.

1. Enter the Pompeu Fabra University campus at c/Ramon Trias Fargas, 25-27. Turn right and walk into a building called Jaume I.

2. Walk confidently past the security desk on a heading of 2 o'clock, to the staircase. Walk down.

3. Immediately to the right is a library. Enter and head for the far left corner.

4. Walk straight on down the corridor in front of you until you come to some stairs going up.

5. Walk up the stairs, go straight on until you come to some doors.

6. Enter, walk forward and around to the left. Tread quietly.

7. Sit down and look up at the building around you.

LA BIBLIOTECA DE LAS AIGUAS
Inside the Universitat Pompeu Fabra
Metro: Ciudatella-Vila Olimpica

SSSH.8.

This is one place where you'll find few tourists and no locals. And that's perfect, because we don't want to share it with anyone. Ignore the hotel bar downstairs and turn right to the lift that goes straight to the roof. It is open to the public, well kind of, better not to ask. But there's a fine bar up there and deckchairs facing the chic boulevard Passeig de Gracia. You kick back, dangle your feet off the edge, gaze at the city laid out in front of you all the way to the ocean and put a sweet smile on your face as the waiter asks you what room number you want to charge your gin and tonic to. Actually, I'd prefer to pay for this in cash, it'll only complicate my room bill. Yes, olives would be lovely, thank you. If you feel really daring you could bring a swimsuit, the small but smart pool is right behind you.

HOTEL MAJESTIC 10th Floor, open 10am-10pm. Passeig de Gracia, 68. Map 5 C4.

HOTEL
MAJESTIC
TERRACE

LA CASETA DE MIGDIA

It's about being close but feeling far away. It's a relaxed bar that throws food on the bbq every now and then, and its location is amazing. Hidden on the far side of the Montjuïc hill, it feels like a beach bar airlifted into a pine tree park. The atmosphere is a hillside Café del Mar – sunset sessions included. And it's still very little known.

HOW TO GET THERE: Go to metro Paral.lel, take the Funicular de Montjuïc (included in your metro ticket), then switch to the cable cars that go up to the castle. From there, walk along with the sea to your left until you come to the Mirador del Migdia – the bar's a little further on, to the right. Or just take a cab to the Mirador del Migdia. Need help? Call Marc, the owner, on 617 956 572.

HOTEL SENATOR SPA

It's the only place round here that you'll find snow in the middle of July. Or a pool filled with oranges. Or a wonderful-smelling eucalyptus sauna. The snow is there for you to roll around in, the fruity pool for you to, well, feel citrusy and the sauna to leave you smelling fresh and tasty for any passing koala bears. In total, the spa contains about ten different sections that you can take at your own pace. Unclench your muscles, clear your mind and pamper your body. It's what weekends are made for.

Hotel Senator Spa. 15 euros for 3 hours, Tuesday to Sunday, 10.30am-2pm or 6pm-10pm c/Cardenal Reig, 11. Tel: 932 609 900. Metro: Collblanc. www.hotelsenatorbarcelona.com

CAFE ESTIU

If you duck 30 seconds off the tourist trail, you can find a quiet little plaza with fountains, goldfish and a beautiful terrace cafeteria to watch the groups of Japanese photography clubs walk unknowingly by.

In front of the Museu Frederic Mares
when the weather gets warm
Metro: Liceo/Jaume I
Map 3 C2

When I leave the bar, I go running up on **Montjüic**. I used to be a marathon runner and that's where I trained.

One restaurant that I love is **Colibrí** on c/Riera Alta, 33 (Tel: 934 423 002; Metro: Universitat). It has a great waiter who treats you really well – and I know a lot about how to treat clients well. They have sensational food.

The majority of my ingredients I buy fresh here in the **Boquería** market, except when I want a particular kind of fish, in which case I send my nephew over to get something special in the trade-only Mercabarna market.

When it's time to go shopping, I visit **Leoni** in Portaferrisa, 13 (Metro: Liceu). It's a classical, elegant shop with exactly the kind of clothes I like.

My favourite place for a cocktail is **Boadas** (c/Tallers, 1; Metro: Catalunya). And in case the young girls ask, I keep a box of Viagra behind my bar.

JOAN (PINOTXO)

OWNS AND RUNS PINOTXO BAR IN THE BOQUERÍA MARKET – AN OLD-TIME CLASSIC OF THE CITY.

Crossing the road into Gracia is like crossing the border out of the city. This is Catalan central, the place to get away from cosmopolitan grandeur and to sit with old people and kids in a quiet, sunny square. There are painted shop fronts and flat-capped men smoking in doorways while groups of square-shouldered women, weighed down with shopping, shout out the day's gossip.

Gracia is a unique mix of the old and the new. The traditions of families that have lived there for generations are mingled with the culture of Catalan youth. Its political vivacity is proudly displayed through the Catalan flags hung over balconies, and the many okupas – squats which have become famous for the political angst they represent. The Movement Okupa is well established, the two most important squats in the area being in c/Ros de Olano and Plaça Rovira i Trias. Keep an eye out, they hold frequent cultural events.

Gracia may also have more bars than any other area, but few have their own dj. These are greasy-tiled bars of old men and strong coffee or

Gracia: a local barrio for local people

airy cafes with home-made cakes and tea. If you wander between them, sooner or later you will come across a square, the focal points of life in Gracia, and which give the place its true appeal.

Each square is different and generates its own particular atmosphere: Plaça del Sol, the most well-known among night-time frequenters, is also the meeting place for sitting in the sun out-side Bar Sol de Nit with a cold beer and a plate of patatas bravas (watch out for the dogs). Elsewhere is Plaça Rius i Taulet, where children run around and the bars put their tables out all over the square. Nou Candan-chú is always packed but worth the wait. Further up at the chilled-out Plaça Virreina, are the mouth-watering offer-ings of the Teashaker bar, while Plaça de la Revoluciò is yet another great place to hang out, especially on Sundays. The streets that criss-cross between the squares are just as intri-guing, hiding boutiques, herb shops and restaurants such as On-li-u in Sant Pere Màrtir, with its heavy fondues and inventive carpaccios. For a relaxing break, St Germain in Torrent de l'Olla is worth a visit for its comfy armchairs and mojitos, while Elephant in Torrent d'en Vidalet offers ground-level relax-ation and an exotic selection of tea in Moroccan glasses.

At the heart of it all is c/Verdi. With an arts cinema and a concentration of restaurants, bars, boutiques and bookshops.

But the charm of Gracia is just in slowly wandering around, a sunny coffee in one quiet square, a tapa in another, getting lost and finding all manner of quiet hidden corners.

eating

Feeding your face
in the city is an art
Get it wrong and you'll
just make a mess

If you are looking for

something filling and greasy for breakfast, you have to know about places like Princesa 23 (whose address is, remarkably, c/Princesa, 23) or The Bagel Shop (c/Canuda) where they'll do you the egg and sausage that your hangover craves.

If you've managed to hang on until lunch (don't peak too early, lunchtime starts at 2pm), you're in for a treat. No matter how busy people are, they will never grab a sandwich and eat it at their desk. The lunch hour (which lasts two hours) is not to be taken lightly. Instead, it's taken heavily every day, and usually with wine. Pretty much the only positive thing that scary dictator Franco ever did for Spain was to reinforce the lunchtime habits of his people. He did this by enshrining in law the Menu del Día. In order that the working man could get a good value lunch without having to go all the way home to his mother, bars and restaurants were forced to offer an all-inclusive cheap set menu. The tradition continues in most places, and some of the classier places in town (such as Biblioteca on c/Junta de Comerç, 28) can suddenly become affordable in the afternoon. Some places even specialise as being

quality restaurants at lunchtime only (such as the quirky

L'economic, Plaça de Sant Agusti Vell).

Prices, quality and portion size vary wildly but there are a few constants: the set menu will include wine or water, coffee or (occasionally and) dessert, and the rest of the place's food is also available if you want to stray from the set dishes. A decent menu will set you back around 8-10 euros a head and you can spend as long as you like enjoying it. If you're near the market on La Rambla, the menus at Bar Iposa (c/Floristes de la Rambla, 14), tucked behind the market, is one of the most reasonable in town if you're not too hungry; if you're starved, try the good value DosTrece on the other side of the children's playground.

But it's in the evening that you see most tourists suffering. Restaurants open at 9pm at the earliest. Brits who usually dine in front of Coronation Street will be struggling – but at least there's always tapas available (Ciudad Comtal is central and very good at the bottom of Rambla Catalunya; and if you like seafood, Bar

Mundial, c/Carders, is a local legend), or you can head to a Basque bar, where they have *pinxos* – snacks on sticks that cost around €1.20 each (try Euskal centre cultural, placeta montcada 1). Keep the sticks – that's what they count to add up your bill.

'**f**' As for evening meals, like any international city, the word of the week is 'fusion'. Catalan fusion, Asian fusion, Modern European fusion (ie. "we don't know what it is either")... the word often means smaller portions and weighty bills. Some manage to do it better than others; Sidecar in the corner of Plaça Reial is surprisingly tasty, for instance. If you're tempted by the huge queues outside Les Quinze Nits in Plaça Reial (they do **reasonable food** at reasonable prices), don't wait in line – instead, go inside and check out the pile of cards referring to the other restaurants in the group. They all do the same kinds of thing and are based in and around the centre.

The real **classy world-shaking** stuff goes on just outside the city centre at Ferran Adria's El Bulli – but unless you're marrying the Prince of Spain, the waiting list is a minimum eight months, which just gives you time to start saving your cash for it. However, those in the know say that Adria's lobster foam is overrated and the real rising star is Ramón Freix Riera at his place El Raco d'en Freix in Zona Alta (c/Sant Elies, 22; Tel: 932 097 559). Waiting lists are also long – but you never know, you might be in luck.

If you want to get down with **the local cuisine** – which mostly consists of different types of sausage, beans, bread and tomato, and well-cooked fish – **genuinely good** Catalan places do exist, you just have to know where to find places like Can Culletes (c/Quintana, 5; Tel: 933 173 022). Or try the pricier Xalet (Avda. Miramar, 31; Tel: 933 249 270 – book ahead) whose view and terrace are unsurpassable. It's hidden next to the Olympic pool up on Montjuïc, where the entire city sits at your feet while you eat.

Tipping rule: Depends on the place. However, serving staff in Spain are generally paid better than their British/American equivalents – 10% is rarely expected.

breakfast at kasparo

breakfast at
ra

If your idea of breakfast

is something more wholesome than a cheap cigarette and an espresso shot strong enough to burn through lead, you might struggle in Catalonia. But then, salvation: two terraces that are the only places to spend a hungry morning. Bar Ra, behind the Boquería market on Las Ramblas, and the Aussie-run Bar Kasparo, tucked in a corner at Plaça Vicenç Martorell near Plaça Catalunya. Both offer fine atmosphere and finer food. Unless, of course, the stomach pixies are going rabid from their near-drowning in alcohol the night before – in which case, only the morning feasts at the Hotel Ritz will do, also available to non-guests. That should do it, at least until lunchtime.

Bar Ra: Plaça Gardunya, Map 4 C4 (Metro: Liceu)
Bar Kasparo: Plaça Vincenç Martorell, Map 4 A3 (Metro: Catalunya)
Hotel Ritz: Gran Via 668 (Metro: Tetuan). Enormous buffet breakfast: €30

mantequeria ravell

Downstairs is one of the most incredible delicatessens in the city. But make it past the hams and the wine, go through the kitchen and up the spiral stairs to find an afternoon restaurant filled with suits who know how to live the good life. The luxurious menu is filled with foie, sauces, fine cuts and flavours that melt in your mouth and leave an impression in your heart. For a post-prandial tipple, whisky lovers will weep at the wall of Scottish names.

c/Aragó, 313
Kitchen open from 10am until 9pm,
except Thurs/Fri (open until 10pm).
Tel: 934 575 114
Metro: Girona

Tapioles, 53

In a hidden restaurant with no name, where every diner has to sign in as a new member of her private club, Sarah explains her food. The finest ingredients from around Europe, described by the Australian chef in loving terms, served in an intimate space shared with a design studio. A very special, home-made experience from start to dessert.

c/Tapioles, 53
www.tapioles53.com
Tel: 93 329 22 38
Metro: Paral.lel

This is the seat for the solo traveler.

To your left: the faces of the locals enjoying their tapas, while others squeeze in to wait for a space. It's quite a show.

In front of them: mountains of fresh mouthwatering tapas – some of the best in the city. There is no menu, you just point at what you like.

In front of you: the chopping board, the hot plate and the smart serving staff as they slice, dice and sizzle to order. From where you're sitting, it's the easiest thing in the world to get their attention, point at anything that looks good – and point back at yourself.

Arrive early and claim your position.

el vaso de oro

c/Balboa, 6 Map 1 A2
Metro: Barceloneta

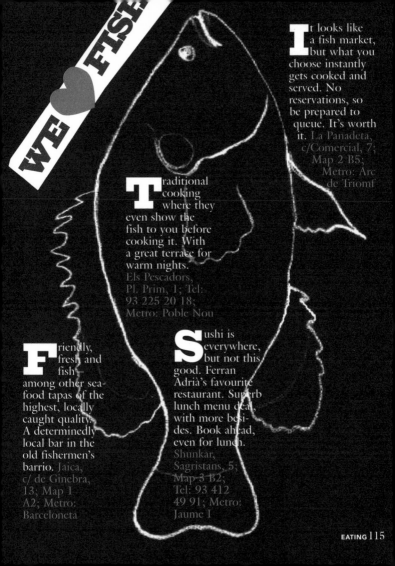

WE ♥ FISH

It looks like a fish market, but what you choose instantly gets cooked and served. No reservations, so be prepared to queue. It's worth it. La Panadeta, c/Comercial, 7; Map 2 B5; Metro: Arc de Triomf

Traditional cooking where they even show the fish to you before cooking it. With a great terrace for warm nights. Els Pescadors, Pl. Prim, 1; Tel: 93 225 20 18; Metro: Poble Nou

Friendly, fresh and fish— among other seafood tapas of the highest, locally caught quality. A determinedly local bar in the old fishermen's barrio. Jaica, c/ de Ginebra, 13; Map 1 A2; Metro: Barceloneta

Sushi is everywhere, but not this good. Ferran Adrià's favourite restaurant. Superb lunch menu deal, with more besides. Book ahead, even for lunch. Shunkar, Sagristans, 5; Map 3 B2; Tel: 93 412 49 91; Metro: Jaume I

bestial

Sophistication, fine food and a side order of the Mediterranean.

C/RAMON TRIAS FARGAS 2-4
METRO: CIUTADELLA-VILA OLÍMPICA
TEL: 932 240 407; MAP 1 B5

NIU TOC Gracia is filled with sunny pavement bars and restaurants – and they're always packed with people. But if you leave the tourist-haunt of Plaça del Sol behind and head to the clumsily-named Plaça de la Revolució de Setembre de 1868, you'll find a little restaurant open at lunchtime. It's called Niu Toc and its fish menu is mighty fine. Sometimes, a calm meal in the Barcelona sunshine can be as precious as the finest cava in town. **METRO: JOANIC; MAP 6 C3**

TEXTIL CAFE

If you want to chill in one of the city's more pleasant courtyards, become a person of the cloth. (If full, turn left out of the Textile Museum and right down an alleyway, where Bar Flassaders has its hidden, sunkissed tables.)

C/MONTCADA, 12; METRO: JAUME I; MAP 2 B3

It's like a cross between a James Bond villain hideout and a New York loft. Chic, stylish and classically Catalan, when the weather's good, there's no view like that from the restaurant at the top of the Barceloneta cable car tower. But if the view doesn't give you vertigo, the price of the food probably will.

Torre de Alta Mar Pg Joan de Borbó, 88. Map 1 D1

Bring your dentist and watch them squirm. Every dish has enough sugar to make a toddler bounce its way to the moon. **Espai Sucre: c/Princesa, 53**
Tel: 932 681 630; Metro: Jaume I. Prices: €25-35 for 5 sweet dishes

Master dessert chefs with their own relaxed gastronomic playground. Let them take your taste buds for a spin.
Dolso c/Valencia, 227; Map 5 B4
Tel: 934 875 964
Metro: Passeig de Gracia

LOVE is in The Air

LOVE
is in The
Air

Pla

Small and in a classical style, tables are intimate, while the fusion menu is as smooth and subtle as a waiter's cough. The atmosphere is perfect for your romantic encounter in the middle of the Gothic. c/Bellafila,5 Map 3 E2; Tel: 934 126 552; M: Jaume I

Limbo

From the superb service to the subtle lighting, this friendly modern restaurant has a way of doing things that you barely even notice. The food melts in your mouth almost as fast as your date. c/Merce, 13 Map 3 E2; Tel: 933 107 699; Metro: Jaume I

Semproniana

The quirky design and old-fashioned style will give you enough to talk about until the main course arrives – by which time the excellent food and wine will be having their warming effect. c/Rosselló, 148 Map 5 B3; Tel: 934 531 820; Metro: Hospital Clinic/Diagonal

is in The Air
is in The Air

SMOOTH COCKTAILS, A **SOPHISTICATED** CLIENTELE AND HUGE PLATES OF SUCCULENT **PASTA** PICKED FRESH FROM THE TREE. CREATED IN THE 1970S, THIS IS ONE OF THE CITY'S MOST **ELEGANT** DESIGN CLASSICS.

IL GIARDINETTO

GRANADA DEL PENEDES, 22

TEL: 932 187 536

FGC STATION: GRACIA

Pretend to be reading the **tortilla** menu while you gaze at the people around you. This has been the place to see and be seen since it opened in 1970. Sunday morning around 12pm gets you the perfect mix of sleepless wide-eyed posh partyers and early-lunching families in this uptown local institution. All under the gaze of the owner's former wife, snapped in her snappy Andy Warhol-style poses.

FLASH
FLASH

C/ LA GRANADA DEL
PENEDES, 25
FGC STATION: GRACIA

la báscula Hidden down a sidestreet in an old candle shop, this is definitely the lunch place you're looking for. Run by an Argentinian collective, Brits in particular will flip sideways at the menu – two pages are devoted to nothing but tea. Hidden behind the counter is a chilled-out café where no two chairs are the same. The menu's just as spritely: big sandwiches, creamy milkshakes, ingredients so fresh that they're still growing, and all in portions that would satisfy a carb-hungry elephant coming off a diet. The food's so good, you forget that it's almost-entirely vegetarian.

Flassaders 30 bis
Mon-Sat 1-11.30pm
Metro: Jaume I
Map 2 B4

also for veggies ——————————————————————→

Organic is hip and hippy with freshly cooked varieties of veg bakes and pizzas.
c/ Junta de Comerc, 1
Metro: Liceu, Map 4 C3

L'illa de Gracia is minimalistic in design, and hearty in portion at lunch and dinner.
c/ St Domenec, 19, Map 6 D1
Metro: Diagonal

Sesamo is trendy, chilled and has great food. Book to avoid disappointment.
c/ St Antoni Abat, 52
Tel: 934 416 411.
Metro: St Antoni; Map 4 B2
www.sesamo-bcn.com

Biocenter is busy, big and full of bio-organic goodies for a filling lunch.
c/ Pintor Fortuny, 25
Metro: Catalunya, Map 4 B3

Templo Hare Krishna is a true city secret, with its own mini-greenhouse right in the Plaça Real. Chilled, hearty, very cheap and bright orange.
Plaça Real, 12 (entresuelo 2a; ring the bell marked Templo)
Metro: Liceu, Map 3 D1

Bodega La Palma Old men walk in, take a glass funnel from the shelf and help themselves from the barrels of wine. Food on offer is a bit of old-style tortilla, maybe some salami, maybe something else if they like the look of you. It's not a tourist spot. It doesn't want to be. While the city has teethed, grown-up, become a sprawling monster, Bodega La Palma has stayed the same way in the same place regardless. But, five generations down the line, word is that this traditional bodega might be soon disappear, probably to make way for a new trendy tapas bar. If you're really interested in Barcelona (and not some flashy, clubby, beach holiday façade), spend a little time here and feel suitably humbled by people who know that the hippest new thing is tomorrow's rotting meat.
c/Palma St Just, 7; Map 3 D2; Metro: Jaume I

Agullers Cal Pep is the lazy journalists' favourite. If you've only got space to mention one tapas bar in your article, it's always this place – which is why it's so packed and touristy. But what they never mention is the family secret: just around the corner is an unimposing bar-restaurant run by Cal Pep's cousin. They trained together, the food is high-quality, the ingredients fresh, the fish melts on your tongue and the prices are low. And you can usually get a table. Keep it under your hat and keep it in the family.
c/Agullers, 8; Map 2 C/D1; Metro: Jaume I

Opaqo You can take anyone to Opaqo – your grandma, your girlfriend, your teenage brother – and they will eat themselves silly. The atmosphere is more about what it isn't. It's not modern fusion or old classic. It's just good, it's friendly and the menu of small dishes is both delicious and good value. The house special, small roast potatoes in a Mallorcan style, have skin that cracks under your teeth as the heat draws the saliva from your glands. With Opaqo, you can never, ever go wrong.
c/Ciutat, 10; Map 3 D2; Metro: Jaume I

Pastafiore, a Barcelona fast food chain, now boasts of 81 different lunch combinations. Here it's chicken with salad or with fries. Or both. Just about as much complexity as I can deal with today. The juiciest flamegrilled chicken in Barcelona and great value, especially the lunch for a fiver deal.

Open 13-01 all days of the year
Llull 32 (con Marina)
Metro: Ciutadella-Vila Olimpica/Bogatell

central catalana del pollastre

When you wake up on that sunny Sunday morning, sore from dancing and drinking, your hair stinks from smoke and your head is bursting from yesterday's adventures, all your body screams for is a calm place, lots of food and another drink. This is your place. Can Martí is hidden among the hills and the food is big and as Catalan as it comes, with lots of charcoaled meat and some veg on the side. The wine goes down as easy as the bill. However, be warned: just finding the place could be one adventure too many. On those particular Sundays, take a taxi.

Ptge de la Font Del Mont, 4
Tel: 934 069 195
Metro: kind of near the Peu del Funicular FGC stop
Closed Mondays and all of August

Turn left at the fruit stall. Take a right when you hit the lingerie. Only the penitent shall pass. Keep going until you hit the heart of the maze, for there you shall find the holy grail. Take a seat at Blanca in the centre of the Mercat St Antoni and enjoy a great lunchtime menu – especially the gazpacho – while you watch the stalls close up around you. It's an island in the centre of an ancient market and the free shot of liquor at the end of your meal may just bring the secret to eternal life.

In the middle of Sant Antoni market
Metro: Sant Antoni
Map 4 B1

OH MAN AREN'T YOU HUNGRY?

Let's buy some food and head to the beach. How about some decent pizza slices at the local classic Pizza Del Born (Passeig del Born 22), Yum, Or maybe a kebab, the juiciest in the city... Kapadokya (Fusteria 8, Map 3 E2). Beef, chicken or a huge range of vegetarian options. More spicy sauce please. Speaking of spicy, Itzli (Mirallers 7, Map 2 B2) does great burritos and nachos. Pure munchie heaven. Though maybe we should go healthy and try the quiches and empanadas at LolaMola (Gignas 28, Map 3 E2). But can we go now please? (All places are Metro: Jaume I)

WHO YOU CALLING UGLY?

Modernism, gothicism, unfinished cathedrals... but the city hides more nooks and crannies for architecture junkies than most reports would have you believe. There's more flavours than a curried fruit salad, some stunning, some deeply ugly – but much of it with its own certain charm.

A lot of the odd bits are products of the country's dictatorship, when architecture was heavily controlled by Franco, who imposed nationalistic references and tried to prevent foreign influence. However, between the 1950s and 1970s, architects reacted with associations like Grupo R, founded by Josep Pratmarsó, while other architects such as **Antoni de Moragas** and **Manuel Baldrich** fought to keep their own particular signature, being inspired by both local and foreign styles. Their battles were not in vain and they left a legacy of exceptional places throughout the suburbs. Everyone goes on about this city and Modernism, but buildings from the 'ugly years' are the work of some of the city's most significant architects and designers and are often unfairly overlooked in favour of their flashier neighbours. We've chosen a few favourites – and the best way to view them is from their atriums.

1950s Residential building
Gran Via 810

The building, designed by Antoni de Moragas during the 1950s, consists of various entrances. To get a better view, cross over to the other side of the street that isn't Gran Via. Then look up. What you'll see is a consecutive series of black and white images of bullfights underneath each of the building's balconies, from the first to the last floor. Raging bulls, rising dust and poised bullfighters swinging their capes. These are the photographs of Francesc Català Roca, **one of Spain's finest** and most important photographers of the 20th century. If you enter the lobby, you can see the photos up close as his macro shots of a bullfighter's costume are displayed as wallpaper along the walls.

1964-1970

The three building complexes contained within this block were planned between 1964 and 1970 by Antoni de Moragas and Francisco Riba de Sales. Their spacious lobbies seem to have a life of their own. Out of the concrete floors rise pillars that extend right across the walls and meet the ceiling beams, intersecting intricate brickwork and tiled ceilings with a bright orange and white pattern. Growing like ivy, small red lamps multiply and branch out from the structural columns, lighting the way towards the exposed central staircase, which is set against yet another wall of patterned tiles. The composition is a mix of international trends and traditional local style.

1973 María cubi building
c/ María Cubi 7-9

Everything you might imagine from the word Kubrickesque. Rounded edges, sleek, seamless surfaces in deep red and bright orange, a ceiling covered by panels of gleaming white disks... retro meets space-age entrance.

1976 Chamber of Commerce
Diagonal 452-454

Once you enter, you'll be swimming in a black marble sea... or drowning in it. Fortunately, the elegant curved staircase sweeps you up from the murky depths and escorts you to safety. Fernando Bendala's use of marble, glass and chrome is reminiscent of the 70s bold, ornamental styles. The Barcelona Centre of Design (BCD) occupies the building's 5th floor.

CLASSIC CINEMAS:
ON THE VERGE OF EXTINCTION

Over the past decade, Barcelona has seen some of its greatest cinemas disappear; some, like the legendary Fémina by Antoni de Moragas, were untimely swallowed by flames. Others, like the Astoria and the Maldà, were gobbled up by real-estate. A few still hold out against the forces of change – but for how long? Admire these survivors, and their remarkable ticket halls, while you still can.

1963 Cine Urgell
Comte d'Urgell 29-33

Perhaps the largest cinema in Spain, Urgell has a stunning vestibule, completed in 1963 by the renowned Antoni Bonamusa.

1969 Cine Rex
Gran Vía 46

Another Bonamusa masterpiece. The ticket clerk looks like she was here before the cinema, and they just built the whole thing around her.

GOTHIC

The Gothic is an area. The Gothic is not an area. Strictly speaking, it's a small part of the old town labelled as such for tax and rubbish collection reasons. But when people talk of 'the gothic', they mean much more. It's the underground river from which Barcelona draws its magic. It's the source of where it began, where it still is, where it's going, away from officially endorsed initiatives and control.

The joy of the Gothic is how it changes from one street to the next, from one doorway to the next, from one floor to the next. Scooters weave along the cobbles and paving in ancient streets. As bits of buildings fell off, other parts were added. A hip boutique sits next to a hippy squat, with an old Catalan bar as its neighbour. As one shop owner

leaves, another fills the space – sometimes more upmarket, sometimes not. The Gothic is always evolving with a reassuring unevenness that gives it a beguiling, confused flavour.

What every part of the Gothic has in common is its ability to lead you round a corner, then another, and then lose you completely. But the maze has several exits and you'll always find yourself on a main thoroughfare – albeit not where you expected.

Every few years, the local government blasts a hole in one section, opening up vast empty squares in the heart of the tiny streets, in an attempt to regulate and organise, pushing with all its might to flatten one side of the balloon. So far, at least, the Gothic is still winning, each time slipping unnoticed from the bulldozers as its secrets seep through the remaining cracks in the paving to where the sunlight never hits and police cars don't quite fit.

Wandering is the best way to find things, but these are our favourites.

C/D'EN BOT. Fall off the tourist traps down this tiny street with a friendly bar at one end, next to the empty square above a space where uncovered Roman tombs sit like discarded teeth in the mud.

C/PARADIS, 10. A thin passageway behind the cathedral where four Roman columns sit like hunting trophies next to the Catalan Exploring Society.

C/BANYS NOUS. A banana-shaped thoroughfare filled with antique shops and old books.

C/AVINYO is the clotted vein of the area, filled with odd shops, odd-smelling side streets and a flush of graffiti (see Shopping).

C/CIUTAT. Duck away from the tourists and explore the maze which includes El Ascensor (enter through ancient elevator doors, c/Belafila,3), the split level Ginger cocktail bar (Palma Sant Just, 1) and cosy Moroccan tea room La Clandestina (c/Viladecols). Roman ruins mark the edges of the zone.

C/CARABASSA. Tucked away off Plaça George Orwell (aka Plaça Trippy due to its reputation as a drug dealer hangout until CCTV was installed), this small street is filled with artists studios and a very good cafe/restaurant Arc Café.

C/MERCÈ AND C/AMPLE. Local bars for local teenagers, but the tapas is good (in the case of Bar Celta La Pulperia, c/Mercè 13, excellent).

ST PERE. St Pere Mes Alt (=top). St Pere Mitja (=middle). St Pere Mes Baix (=bottom). The street names say it all – this is not an area that was created with much thought.

It's determinedly local, in the centre but devoid of tourist attraction (bar the shortbread tin Palau Musica Catalana), peopled by old Catalans and young immigrants from Central America and South Asia.

Tucked away are some great bars (Gluh, Carlos) squeezed into the tiny street Verdaguer i Callis, a miniature museum of magic (c/Oli 6, only open Thursdays 6-8pm and for a weekly magic show on Sundays at 12pm) and, between c/Fonollar and c/Jaume Giralt, an ugly vacuum of space thrust into the maze, where neo-futurist housing stares at the bare skeletons of former flats, their walls a patchwork of old wallpaper. A temporary park of bike wheels, plant pots and benches sits in the void, built by the residents to fill the hole left by the developers.

Plaça St Agust Vell is a pretty little square with a couple of bars, including Bar Mundial's excellent tapas and remarkable collection of old boxing photos. Hidden in one corner is L'Economic, a great local lunch spot. The elderly landlady taking your order painted all of the pictures.

THE BORN. Ten years ago, the Born was where you wouldn't take your kids. Now it's a tourist centre, with cool bars, expensive artist studios, posh restaurants and over-priced apartments. It's also a great place to hang out in the sun.

c/Banys Vells is a small street hidden behind the St Maria del Mar church, and is a very good place to dine. La Havana Vieja and El Pebre Blau are two worthy options.

Keep an eye on the Convent Sant Agusti in c/Comerç – this remarkable former convent often hosts a market, dj or some random cultural event.

I've been living in c/Petrixol my entire life. I love that street. It's one of the oldest in Barcelona and is known as **the chocolate street.** The entire population of Catalonia goes down there to have a hot chocolate with churros.

For breakfast, if I have the time I go to the **Boqueria market** on Las Ramblas and have something at Pinotxo or Quim, who do quite heavy breakfasts: fried eggs with fried small fish, meatballs with cuttlefish, things like that – lots of energy for the day. For a quick breakfast I usually buy something at **Xocoa** (c/Petritxol, 11).

Some of my lunch favourites are **Cal Pep** (Plaça de les Olles, 8; Metro: Barceloneta) and an Italian called **Locanda**, just off Via Laeitana (c/Doctor Joaquim Pou, 4; Metro: Jaume I). **Santa Maria** (c/Comerç, 17; Metro: Barceloneta) is also very good, as is **Shunka**, a Japanese restaurant that some say is the best in town (c/Sagristans, 5; Metro: Jaume I). **Can Majó** (c/Almirall Aixada, 23; Metro: Barceloneta) does great paellas.

For an evening meal, **Pla** is cool (c/ Bellafila, 5; Metro: Jaume I) and **Noti** (c/Roger de Llúria, 35; Metro: Passeig de Gracia) just changed their cook and the place is really beautiful. **Torre de Alta Mar** (see Eating) is good too – I like especially their seafood.

Afterwards I'd go to **Club13** (Placa Real,13; Metro: Liceu) where I dj sometimes, to **Macarena** (c/Nou de Sant Francesc 5; Metro: Drassanes) or maybe up to **Hotel Florida** (Carretera Vallvidrera, 83-93; see Sleeping). They have some great views from up there.

MARC ESCURSELL OWNS CLOTHES SHOP SO_ DA AND IS ONE OF THE PEOPLE BEHIND XOCOA, A LOCAL CHAIN OF STYLISH CHOCOLATE SHOPS.

drinking

Alcohol is ever-present in the city. From the morning shot of rum or whisky in your coffee, via the carafe of wine with a lunchtime meal to a quiet small beer after work, just because the Spanish tend not to maraud through the centre stealing traffic cones and wearing plastic breasts, that's not to say their livers aren't as shot as everyone else's. Local peculiarities include the traditional glass of cava with the family on Sundays and various bars that specialise in absinthe tourist favourite Marsella on c/Sant Pau 65, Metro Liceu, is a local favourite too, though Barcelona Rouge (p.152) also does a mean selection of absinthe cocktails). Still others serve teenage drinking favourite "leche de pantera"

ing

It means 'panther's milk' and is served in bars on c/Mercè – just ask around. It comes in unmarked bottles from under the counter, and you don't realise quite how strong it is until you try and stand up. That's not calcium that's making **your knees wobble**. If you find yourself out beyond closing (3am for bars) and not keen on paying to go to a club, there's always the beer sellers on Las Ramblas, a thoughtful public service provided mostly by people of Pakistani origin, and one that never seems to **dry.**

sitting
way

up

here
people
look
like

tiny

ants
m
wa
ha
ha
ha

MIRABLAU
PLAÇA DOCTOR ANDREU
NEXT TO THE TIBIDABO FUNICULAR

Muebles Ciudad

The concept of used furniture has been taken all the way in Barcelona. Muebles Ciudad took it even further by converting a furniture store into a stylish bar. Comfy sofas, good-looking crowd, smooth cocktails, finger food and an open wifi connection... you could end up spending hours there at any time of the day or night. They also offer a platform for upcoming artists on behalf of Somos, a multidisciplinary arts agency whose office is just above the bar.

c/Ciudad, 5; Metro: Jaume I; Map 3 D2

If you enjoy a good swill and a spit, there are few places
more fruitywithanoaksmokedhintofautumn than D.O.
Just reading the wine selection is enough to give you gout.
A wine bar that feels more like a friendly cafe, if you
accompany your choice with chunks of their fresh parmesan,
wine drinking will never be the same again.

c/Verdi, 36; Map 6 B3
Metro: Gracia

QUIMET & QUIMET

There's an old song from the States that goes "I left my heart in San Francisco". Well, in a small box behind the bar at Quimet & Quimet sit my taste buds. There's no tapas bar like it. Everything is wrong – it's expensive but it's not in the centre. It serves the finest wines and whiskies to a local crowd, not a room full of suits. They make tapas from smoked fish and the most incredible flavours kept in a jar... but they don't make a big thing of it. They just do what they do, and they do it better than anyone else.

c/Poeta Cabanyes, 25; Map 5 D2
12-4pm, 7-10.30pm.
Metro: Paral.lel

TRY WEDNESDAYS FROM 10 PM.
(IT FILLS MORE AT THE WEEKEND)

What you don't want is the atmosphere. Instead → you want to arrive with all of your friends and make them smile... HINT: adding arrows to the barstaff as they pour → your drinks is unlikely → so you can have a target all to yourselves → the place is empty → so you can... I hope the atmosphere...

L'AR QUER

L'ARQUER. c/GRAN VIA, 454. Metro: ROCA FOR...

As Raval gets redeveloped (see p30), a lot of the dirty charm may leave, but at least some good bars are filling the vacuum. Within five minutes of each other are three great places to start the night, and one to continue. **Ambar** (Sant Pau, 77) is the largest, with a few sofas along the walls and large windows facing Rambla del Raval. **Bar 68** (Sant Pau, 68) is a straightforward cosy place with a small upstairs where you can tuck yourself away. Smallest, and craziest, is **Sifo** (Espalter, 4), where the room at the back gets loud and wild. Then follow it up with a dance in **Zentraus** (Rambla del Raval, 41), a small club that closes at 3, with more unusual music tastes, mainly on the electronic scale, and is open every night of the week. Sometimes even gentrification has its good side.
METRO: LICEU (ALL MAP 3 C/D3)

Hidden away in unfashionable Poble Sec are two of the city's funkier secrets. For a lazy night on the comfy chairs, there's Barcelona Rouge, a laid-back cosy bar (when the football's not on) where you can sip an absinthe cocktail with a partner or friends and happily wave goodbye to the evening.

Barcelona Rouge
c/Poeta Cabanyes, 21; Metro: Paral.lel

A few streets away behind a heavy metal door is Mau Mau – an old warehouse, now converted into a quiet lounge club for members (anyone can join). Sit on the huge red sofas and enjoy its chilled soul djs. Best night: Thursdays in the warm-up for their night The Powder Room, just around the corner at the club Sala Apolo.

Mau Mau c/Fontrodona, 33
www.maumaunderground.com

Who's there?

Everything or nothing – it depends on how good you are at talking your way in. There are the secret bars, the bells you ring or the doors you tap, but admittance is restricted to friends, friends of friends, and those deserving enough to pass the doorman. This could be the best night of your life or a five-second shrug and a face full of splinters. (Caribbean Club and Kiriki are the most forgiving)

Cow Bar – c/Milans; look for the cow sign
Metro: Jaume I Map 3 D/E2
Kiriki – c/Banys Vells, 13
Metro: Jaume I Map 2 B3
Caribbean Club – c/Sitges, 5
Metro: Catalunya Map 4 A3/4
Papillon – a small street off c/Princesa
Ask around, but only after 3am
Metro: Jaume I

down on one of the sofas, call over a four euro cocktail and enjoy an atmosphere as chilled as a penguin in a ice bucket. Retro seventies meets your own front room in the perfect place to sit with friends and talk away the world.
Bodega Kenobi
c/Notariat, 7
Map 4 B4
Metro: Catalunya
Wed, Thurs 7-11pm
Fri-Sun 7-2am

When I look into your eyes, I'm lost. My skin tingles and, giddy, I fall. The bubble is sealed, the blindfold is on and I can't sense an outside beyond the flick of your lashes and the eternity of your green-flecked stare. In every other bar, it was me and you, us sitting in a place, watching the people and sipping our drinks. But here in this quiet, elegant, wood-glow jazz-slow corner we have found a spot tucked under the stairs and the world has gone away for the night. Here we are in our place you and me utterly lost in each others' eyes.
Les Gens que J'aime
c/Valencia, 286 (by Passeig de Gracia); Map 5 B4
Metro: Diagonal

toscano antico

Toscano Antico is not a sophisticated cocktail bar. The barmen are rowdy, the space is small, and if you arrive before 10pm, you can help yourself to the free tapas on the bar. Then you take a look at the cocktail list. You didn't even know half those things were drinks. But you know that feeling when you go to a weird party where you're a friend of a friend and you really don't want to go along but you eventually get persuaded and everything looks kinda weird until three hours later when you suddenly realise that you're having one of the best nights of the year? Toscano Antico serves that by the glass.

c/Aribau 167; Metro: Diagonal; Map 5 B3.

You could arrive in a smoking jacket and still feel underdressed.
Dry Martini is James Bond, it's Lauren Bacall, it's Cary Grant.
Smooth and slick as a vaseline ice-rink, this bar is so sophisticated
it makes royalty blush. Whether you're downstairs with your
secretary, at the huge table in the secret Speak Easy restaurant
making an offer they can't refuse, or perched by the bar as the
artists in white jackets paint liquid into a glass, this is the kind of
place where Frank and JFK are toasting us from on high.

martini

c/Aribau, 162; Metro: Diagonal; Map 5 A3; Tel: 932 175 072; www.drymartinibcn.com

Down at the dark end of town are three of the city's small-space big-heart old-time favourites. Start at **Pastis**, a small wooden locker in the old French style, where live music drips down the walls, the guitarist squeezed into a corner next to the toilets. Then slide around to **La Concha**, where Sara Montiel (aka Spain's

LA CONCHA
BAR PASTIS
EL CANGREJO

Audrey Hepburn) grins demurely at a pleasantly gay bar with a Moroccan vibe. End up at **El Cangrejo**, across the road – loud, proud and unashamedly fresch on Friday and Saturdays, with space to dance and a flamboyant, low budget, in-your-face attitude that's perfect for those in a mood to match. Sunday nights bring forward Carmen de Mairena, a transsexual with a cabaret show that's truly something. We're not sure what, but it's surely something and there's nothing quite like it anywhere else.

Pastis: c/Santa Mònica, 4
La Concha: c/Guàrdia, 14
El Cangrejo: c/ Monsterrat, 9B
Metro: Drassanes Map 4 D/E3

DON'T WORRY

ABOUT THE BELGIAN **WORRY** REINTERPRETATION OF HAMLET THROUGH THE MEDIUM OF MIME GOING ON IN THE MAIN HOUSE.

THE BAR IS OPEN FOR ALL.

ITS HIPPY CHIC IS FUN, BUT THE HIGHLIGHT IS THE BACK YARD — QUIRKY, SPACIOUS, AND IN THE SUMMER, A WONDERFULLY HIDDEN PLACE TO HAVE A DRINK.

L'ANTIC TEATRE

Verdaguer i Callis, 9

Metro: URQUINAONA

ESPai rAi

If Barcelona truly is the new Parisian Left Bank, its heart isn't in the opera houses or the officially sanctioned festivals, but in spaces like Espai Rai. The small bar is a buzz of different languages, the art is weird, the free internet used liberally and the monthly cabarets at the end of each month are an odd delight, no matter what your mother tongue is. There's also international films shown every Thursday. Open "almost" every day from 10am to 10pm, if you can find its hidden entrance (next to a big-windowed bar; it usually it has the film timetable pasted onto it), it's the place to go if you want to hang with the city's arty underground.

Espai Rai
Carders 12
Metro: Jaume I

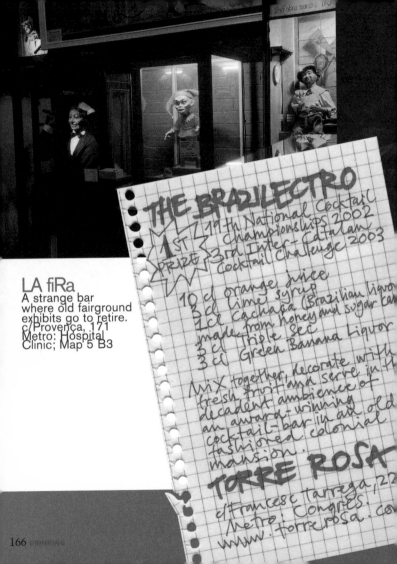

LA fiRa
A strange bar
where old fairground
exhibits go to retire.
c/Provença, 171
Metro: Hospital
Clinic; Map 5 B3

THE BRAZILECTRO
1ST PRIZE 11th National Cocktail
Championships 2002
3rd Inter-Catalan
Cocktail Challenge 2003

10 cl orange juice
3 cl lime syrup
3 cl Cachaça (Brazilian liquor
made from honey and sugar cane
1 cl Triple Sec
3 cl Green Banana Liquor

Mix together, decorate with
fresh fruit and serve in the
decadent ambience of
an award-winning
cocktail-bar in an old
fashioned colonial
mansion.

TORRE ROSA
c/Francesc Tarrega, 22
Metro: Congres.
www.torrerosa.co

When the cars parked on the road change from Seats to Porsches, you know you're getting close to **Premiere**. The age range is mixed, but the wallets are equally well-endowed at this relaxed cocktail bar with a small upstairs, where beanbags and two mattresses await the world weary. Lively, wealthy and colourful, it's a good place to take a partner who likes the view to be good looking and well dressed.

c/Provença 236; Map 5 B3
www.barpremier.com
Metro: Diagonal

Sometimes, when it's raining and cold, all you want is somewhere warm to curl up in a ball for the day. Instead of your own bed, go to a welcoming bar with beds of their own. **La Fianna** may be full of local-living Americans and Brits, but its cushion-filled platforms are the best place to sit and order drinks/food all day long. They also do a mean Sunday brunch. If you tire of there, head to **Kashbah.** Alongside the Museum of the History of Catalunya is an unlikely location for a cool little bar with funky djs, cushion-filled corners, North African rugs and movie nights on Wednesdays. All we have to do is wait for this goddam sun to go away.

La Fianna: c/Banys Vells, 15;
Map 2, B3; Metro: Jaume I

Kashbah: Palau de Mar; Map 1, A2;
Metro: Barceloneta

La Garrafa dels Beatles

Thirty years old and no less strange than it was on day one, Joan and Ricky's bar is in a quiet, local area where no tourists tread, and is a shrine to all things Fab Fourish. From real Cavern Club sawdust to a copy of John Lennon's marriage certificate, the decor in this strange bar is hardly subtle. Documentaries and concert footage play on the screens, and, every single night, they put on **a mini-gig of their favourite hits.** The only trouble is, after thirty years of doing it, they still don't know all the words.

c/Joan Güell, 150
Metro: Les Corts
www.thebeatles-pub.com

Zona Alta

is a world in itself. Essentially a series of areas just below the hills at the back of the city, this is where money lives and money stays. The city is less than half an hour away, but it could be on the other side of the Mediterranean as far as 95% of the people in Pedralbes, Sarrià and St Gervasi de Cassoles are concerned. The rich Catalan families have their shops here, their bars, their restaurants, their night clubs. There are few tourists, even fewer immigrants, and this is the way they like it. It's mostly old money, where a small flat on c/Ganduxer or around Turó Park will have a starting price of around €1m. The families all own houses down the coast and in the summer will head there for the weekends. With small squares, closed groups and sophistication that you can't teach, this is Barcelona's Notting Hill. If the people here shop, they head for the labels on c/Tenor Viñas, where a shopping centre is flanked by upmarket stores like Rosa Hojas and E4G. If they go out, they have cocktails at Gimlet (c/Santaló 46), Elefant (Passatge dels Til·lers, 1) or any of the many bars around c/Marià Cubí, before going to Sutton Club (c/Tuset 13) – where they'll have a VIP card, naturally. The most exclusive food is sold at the delicatessen Semon (c/Ganduxer, 47) who supply royal weddings, Paradís (Psg Manuel Girona, 23) and the bakery Sacha (Plaça Adriano). Eating out could be at the classical Mariona (c/Amigó, 53; Tel: 932 011 830) or Can Punyetes (c/Marià Cubí, 189; Tel: 932 009 159). If you want to do some fantastic people-watching among the better-than-thou (and you can't talk your way into the Barcelona Polo Club on Avenida Pedralbes, 16 or the Club Tennis Barcino, Plaça Narcisa Freixa, 2-3) head for Turó Park and the tapas bars on c/Mandri, such as Marlin, Pescadito and Bar Mandri. Or, if it's a Sunday, why not go to church and see the rich wives try to outdo each other while the teenagers flirt. Once all that's all done, head for Mare de Déu de la Bonanova in Plaça Bonanova for some calm reflection among the far-from-meek.

'm from Barcelona, and have always lived here. It's a city that combines **social harmony** and tradition with modern and multicultural youth.

The gallery is about showcasing artists that we like and that we believe have been **overlooked**. We like diverse styles and projects – despite the name, we're not just about pop art. We're really lucky that Barcelona has become such a great city for more unconventional artists. I just hope that the local government doesn't spoil it too much with all their new **pro-civic' laws**.

On a perfect day, I would drink a coffee at **Mirablau** (Plaça Doctor Andreu). Then I'd do a route of my favourite galleries, such as **Coldcreation** (Aragón 379), **ADN** (Enric Granados 49), **Lluciâ Homs** (Consell de Cent 315), la **Galeria dels Àngels** (carrer dels Àngels 16), **KBB** (Joaquin Costa 42) and **Miscelänea** (Guardia 10). Then I'd go shopping at **RAS** (Doctor Dou 10), **Loring Art** (Gravina 8), **Bingo Shop** (Roger de Lluria 45), **Freaks** (Ali Bei 10) and the **Mercado Del Borne** (Rec 37-9) to look at books and satisfy my design fetishes.

I'll eat something in the **Santa María** restaurant next to the gallery (Comerç 17), have a drink in **Casa Paco** (Allada Vermell 10) and then maybe end up in **El Indie** in Raval (Guardia, 15). A superfreaky place filled with everyone from transvestites to mods.

I'll also try to go to visit an artist in their studio – I just **love** the smell of fresh paint.

IÑIGO RUNS THE IGUAPOP GALLERY
C/COMERC 15, AND HE HATES HAVING HIS PHOTO TAKEN.

173

Barcelona may not be perfection, but it has pretty much perfected the art of the music festival. Where else could you enjoy one of the best indie-pop festivals on the continent, and then witness the world champions of electronic weirdness just a couple of miles and a few days down the road? Not too long ago, this town was culturally dozing, stirring briefly and predictably only in the warmth of the summer sun. Then suddenly, as if from nowhere, a number of different international influences met on the beach, had a few beers together, shared a cab home and the musical party began. From the miniscule to the enormous, the rabidly modern to the unashamedly retro, the jaw-dropping to the ear-bleeding, the local music festival calendar is packed full of unmissable events. **The three big boys are** Sonar, Primavera Sound **and** BAM. Sonar **www.sonar.es, or** El Festival Internaciónal de Música Avanzada **to use its Sunday name, has become the essential pilgrimage for European dance music. For three days in June, the empty concrete gap between the** MACBA **and** CCCB **museums gets some fake grass, a few tents and is transformed into the planet's coolest chillout space to enjoy the most challenging and fresh electronic music from around the globe, and pro-bably beyond. At night, the whole thing decamps to a warehouse on the outskirts of town, where big names (Bjork, Massive Attack, etc) keep the crowds jumping. The evening venue can feel a bit corporate, and many connoisseurs buy Day tickets**

only, spending the night at one of the alternative music festivals that coincide with the main event, such as OffSonar, Algorhythm or Sala Apolo's Versus. But music isn't just about playing with PowerBooks. A mere five years in, and Primavera Sound www.primaverasound.com has become the main city-based, indiekid rockout in Spain. With its own campus at the Forum venue by the seashore, and acts like Lou Reed, the Pixies, the Fall, PJ Harvey and more Spanish rock than you can shake a fist at, it's a loud, fun time for everyone.
Also at the Forum is BAM, a huge free indie festival supporting local bands (and throwing in a few stars too) at the end of September www.bam.es.
More indies are on show at LEM in Gracia www.gracia-territori.com, in the all-Spain touring festival Wintercase in the winter, and Summercase... you can probably work that out for yourself www.wintercase.com. And if you don't mind travelling out of the city a little, keep an eye on the dates for FEA (electroclash) in Les Basses, FISC (punk from around the world) in Santa Coloma, Hipersons for all your modern Catalan thrash favourites, and, when you've had enough of guitars, there's always Terrassa's international jazz festival in the spring, Barceloneta's flamenco in the summer, Badalona and Cerdanyola's blues fests, Vilanova i la Geltru's own world music gathering... and so on. In Barcelona, the beat goes on, in all of its forms. So hit the streets, read the flyers and above all, keep your ears open.

GOING

You dancin'? Cos we're askin' and we're also sayin' that this is a city where getting your freak on is practically compulsory.

If you really want to show yourself ahead of the game, you'll go out on Thursdays and Sundays, where crowds are smaller and music offerings more select. But if the weekend for you is when the sun never rises, here's some places to head (and don't even think about hea-

ding there before 2am).

If the new rock scene is your thing, the barrio of Poble Nou, further along the beach and beyond, is for you. It's a semi-abandoned industrial neighborhood that city officials are trying to give a Miami-style facelift. It holds many of the real underground venues and parties. Although the Ruler of the Night in the area is Razzmatazz (see following pages), there are plenty of other places close by. For high-energy electro rock, there's concert space The Factory (Sancho de Ávila, 78; www.thefactorybcn.com), but for the real authentic underground thing and a late crowd visit Caribe, (Espronceda, 166; www.amicsdel carib.blogspot.com), a hidden second-floor bar that you enter through a small door and climbing the stairs next to the bar entrance. The street Marià Cubí (and those around it) is Uptown, an upper-class hang out with few tourists and lots of rich kids, based around

OUT

a street of the same name that's filled with bars and a few places for later as well. The Mas i Mas Bar there (Marià Cubí,199) is an island of RnB/funk in a sea of europop, with bar-club Universal across the street. Some uptowners will then head to Otto Zutz (Lincoln, 15) with its late closing and flyers in pretty much every bar (but don't count on a short walk home). For variety, they may go to reasonably lively Zac Club (Avda. Diagonal, 477; Metro: Hospital Clínic) or to the disco-glam Sutton Club (Tuset, 13; Metro Diagonal), where more than 1000 people have VIP cards – the best place in town for observing interbreeding and posh totty. When they head downtown, it's to BARcelona (aka Buddha Bar) at c/Pau Claris, 92, known for its Models Night parties on Tuesdays. Meanwhile, Vila Olympica by the beach is the new hideout for the fashionistas. A few years ago it was something of a post-Olympic ghost town, but now there's the highly fashionable CDLC (Psg Maritim 32. Metro Ciudatella-Vila

Olímpica; Sunday night is achingly trendy night) and Shoko two floors down. If you tire of the bar-club vibe, the Catwalk Club is just round the corner (Ramon Trias Fargas, 2-4; www.clubcatwalk.net) for warehouse-style dancing with some decent djs on the decks. Then head to the beach to sleep it off. Places downtown that merit a mention: City Hall (Rambla Catalunya 2-4, just north of Plaça Catalunya) brings in good house DJs and is right in the centre of town. It also has a chill-out terrace for those sweltering summer nights. Just off Las Ramblas, on one side you have pre-party flirting location Café Royal (Nou de Zurbano, just off Plaza Real), and on the other side is Moog (Arc del Teatre, 3; Metro: Liceu; www.masimas.com), the main venue for techno-

heads to bounce their way through the small hours. Club Fellini (Las Ramblas, 27,www.clubfellini.com) is the all-year-round club from the people behind La Terrrazza (see following pages) with a decent enough line-up, plus killer metal-pop riffs on their Nasty Mondays. On the other side of Raval, just off a wide street called Paral.lel, is Sala Apolo (c/Nou de la Ramla, 113; Metro: Paral.lel; www.sala-apolo.com), a multi-personalitied location where Wednesdays are international films, Thursdays are funk, weekends are concerts and clubbing. And if you prefer your locations unpretentious, cheap, central, small and defiantly local, there's always La Macarena (Nou de Sant Francesc, 5; Metro Liceu; free before 2.30am), which fortunately has no relation whatsoever with the Euro dance (s)hit of the same name.

LA PALOMA

It was just another day in Metropolis. But suddenly, mild-mannered geriatric 1920s ballroom dancing hall *La Paloma* hears a cry for a club that's a decent size; for some decor that's not just yet another trendy bar with a dance floor. *A few hours and one swift lighting change later and* it becomes LA PALOMA, a huge 100 year-old nightclub with the power and groove to strike fear into the heart of its mortal enemies. Only the chandelier, paintwork and the nature of the building give away its alter-ego.

Tigre, 27. Open during the week as an old time dance hall. **Open Thursdays / Fridays / Saturdays as a night club.** metro: universitat. **www.lapaloma-bcn.com**

This is as close to Ibiza-style clubbing you will ever get in Barcelona. **La Terrrazza** has brought in the best deejays for the last 10 years, and even though the place has seen better days, the venue is still magic. If you like happy, open-air clubbing, this is your choice.
Poble Espanyol Metro: Espanya (and then a 15-minute walk up Montjuïc)
Open every summer, www.laterrrazza.com

Danzatoria, above the city on Avenida Tibidabo 61 is an amazing mansion house in the hills, with a restaurant upstairs, a dance floor downstairs and a **stunning gard** filled with the young and the beautiful. It's not as 'in' as it u to be, but still well worth a visit. The afternoon session on

Sundays in the summer are a highlight of the year. Look to leave by 2.30am for a chance of getting a taxi. In an even more elegant uptown mansion is **Elephant** (Ptge dels Til·lers, 1). Located in Pedralbes, this is the hang out for the rich and semi-famous. A three-storey villa surrounded by a garden, with the obligatory VIP room, this can be the place to see and be seen.

A massive building with German industrial chic, **Razzmatazz** is five clubs in one. The Loft and Sala Lolita are for the club crowd, RazzClub is a point of reference for live music, Pop Bar is the home of eclecticism and the Temple Beat Room is the place for soul and rap vibes. One ticket, one huge space, something for absolutely everyone. Fridays, Saturdays 1-5am; c/Almogávers, 122 (Loft and Lolita: enter in c/Pamplona, 88); Metro: Marina; www.salarazzmatazz.com

JAZZ SÍ

Every day is DIFFERENT at Jazz Sí. Be you rocker, flamenco, Cuban or jazz, **THIS TINY HIDDEN** space belonging to the music school already **HAS YOU** figured out.

Mon, Weds, Sat: Jazz; Tues, Sun: Rock; Thurs: Cuban; Fri: Flamenco. Starts between 8 and 9pm (Sun 6.30pm). Free entry if you buy a drink. Requesens, 2 Map 4 B2; Metro: Sant Antoni. www.tallerdemusics.com

Barcelona is not known for its hip-hop – or for any type of music apart from electronic dance. But if grooves are your thing, you could head to Gracia and check out **Garrito** (c/Vic; Metro: Fontana) and then **Clase** (c/Francisco Giner; Metro: Diagonal), THE place hang out with the graffiti kids and the hip-hop heads. As for clubs, the original crib **Jamboree**. It may be in tourist central (Plaça Real; Metro: Liceu) but it keeps it real with the mainstream tunes, especially on a Monday. For the more chilled side of funky, head to **Mau Mau** (c/Fontrodona 3 Metro: Paral.lel) on Thursdays before continuing the night a the nearby **Sala Apolo's** Powder Room.

hip HOP

THE CITY NEVER SLEEPS

If you're a dedicated clubber/chemical substance aficionado the best time of the week is when your sweaty half-naked body is rubbing against others, all smiling, caressing and feeling that special chemical closeness. This is a great city for after-hours. You can find more options than these here but venues are usually small and locations keep changing, so look out for flyers when leaving clubs. Entry is about 20-25 euros, discount flyers exist but guest lists are rare. These are our favourites this year:

Souvenir (c/Noi del Sucre, 75, Viladecans; taxi from the centre: approx €25-30) is still the best 'after' around. It has a mixed crowd (though more queer than straight) just outside the city, and the music is mainly positive house. There are free buses from outside Poble Espanyol when the clubs close and then back to the centre of town. It lasts from around 6am until 2pm. Best day is Sunday mornings.

Right next to Souvenir you have **Merci** (c/ Llobatona, 50) a newish venue that caters to a more straight-straight crowd. It starts at 6am and goes on all day. Hip cats say that it's a no-go for them, but it can be fun with the right people.

Bang Bang, in the centre of the city (Gran Via, 580, on the corner of Muntaner) is a small and popular option for the more casual, once-in-a-while crowd. The atmosphere is more personal and the music is slightly softer, attracting a good crowd.

And for those with enough energy or substance on Monday mornings head to **La Luna** (Av. Diagonal 323). The madness is out there, if only you can find it.

MUNCHIES

Something of a local legend, the croissant factory churns out butterfilled breads for drunken punters at the bargain price of €2 for a boxful. (They always outlast the night and they never taste quite so good in the morning.) c/Lancaster – follow your nose. Metro: Liceu

If the apocalypse comes, **Bar Paris** will be serving patatas bravas to the horsemen. We're not sure if this place ever shuts. It's an old time student favourite, a bit of a trek from the gothic area, but with the greasy sandwiches your stomach gremlin is roaring out for. On the corner of c/Paris and c/Aribau. Metro: Hospital Clinic

El Reloj is open late (or is it early?) on weekends and has the advantage of being fairly central. The food's great post-club at 6am (but we're not sure if we'd try it at any other time) Via Laietana, 40; Metro: Jaume I.

There are lots of skate spots. For instance, the square with the chimneys by **c/de Cabanes** and **Avinguda de Paral.lel** (Metro: Paral.lel), plus in front of the **MACBA** museum, **Plaça dels Països Catalans** in front of Sants station and at the **port**; there's a new extension where the ferries leave for the Balearic islands – and it's a perfect skating area.

I also like to go riding in old pools, ramps etc. **Mataró Park** has a new space. But our aim is to create a skate park in **Montjuïc**, behind the Olympic stadium. It should be finished by summer 2006.

The snowboard scene is great. Three hours and you're in the mountains. We go to **Andorra** or to **La Molina** – it's basic but there's snow. One morning, I went boarding until 11am, got into the car knowing there were good waves in Barcelona and three hours later I was riding a wave.

The post-board scene all happens downtown, on **c/Nou de la Rambla** and below. The key place is **Bar Manolo** (c/Lancaster, 3; Metro: Liceu). When the pro-riders come to town, they all end up drinking there. Another really cool bar is **Kentucky** (c/Arc del Teatre, 11; Metro: Liceu). Then there's **Fonfone** and **Shanghai**, both next to each other on and near c/Escudellers (Metro: Drassanes). But Monday is always **Jamboree** night (Plaça Reial; Metro: Liceu).

As for eating, as you know, skaters have no money so restaurants are not a big issue – but one place that usually works is **Pizza del Born** (Passeig del Born, 22; Metro: Jaume I), for cheap and good pizza. **Milk** (Correos) is a great bar/restaurant where a lot of the guys hang out too. But in the winter, you'll find us all surfing down at the beach. The waves are best then.

SOREN MANZONI
WORKS FOR SKATEBOARD BRAND
BURTON AND ALSO DJS

dr ug s

don't think you're hallucinating if you can smell dope. It's not legal but in some bars it feels like it. Barcelona's an open-minded city in a rebellious region of a country that shares a sea border with Morocco. When you think about it, it's amazing any work gets done beyond constantly going out for munchies.

What most people are doing is smoking pot. There are protests, petitions and discussion groups to try and legalise it, but so far they've haven't got anywhere. However, it's not just for the underground scene. This isn't Amsterdam, but it's still pretty normal to see a spliff in the street, in one of the chilled bars that still allows smoking of any kind, and especially in the parks at the weekend.

The law's a bit fuzzy about possession (dealing is obviously going to land anyone in jail faster than you can say 'pssst'). At the time of writing, it's actually legal to carry small amounts "for personal use", whatever that means. A recent court case showed that it's really very small indeed.

The way things are is this: if you have a

spliff and want to light up, see if anyone else is smoking first. If not, just ask at the bar if you can. They won't mind – they're probably asked several times a night and they won't throw you out or call the cops if the answer is 'no'. The question you want to ask is "Se puede fumar porros?" (Porros = joints. María = marijuana. Hashish is what you think it is, and is the most common form of dope available).

s for getting hold of the stuff, the shadows of the major tourist hang-outs like Plaça Reial, Plaça Catalunya and sidestreets near Las Ramblas are filled with scary types with things to sell, but we really wouldn't if we were you. Stick to daytime and the parks – follow your nose and ask anyone with a smile. But beware of what they hand over, as people have been known to sell shredded liquorice or chocolate, and at a premium price.

There are also more than 40 'grow shops' in Barcelona that sell hemp seeds, but don't go marching in asking where to buy the developed stuff – they value their shop licence too much. If you want to visit one and hang out with like-minded people, try Qhiria on c/ Mila i Fontanals, 35 (Metro: Joanic). They have djs on Fridays, reggae on Wednesdays and

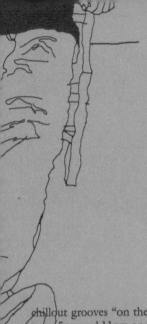

chillout grooves "on the rug" between 5pm and 11pm on Sundays. There's harder stuff around too, of course. You can tell just by walking into any club – spot the people dancing with their jaws. City favourites include coke and speed (often cut with caffeine pills, mannitol or ephidrine). Designer drugs have also hit the night scene, as has GHB, alongside acid and pills.

If you want to buy, you probably already know what to look out for – the dealers hang around the same kinds of nightclub corners here as in any other Western country. But, like anywhere else, there's no guarantee of what you're buying – even less for a tourist than a local, who would find it easier to track the dealer down later if there's a problem.

PRICES IN SUMMER 2006 (in €, per gram) cocaine: 60, crystal: 60, MDMA: 60, Special K: 60. One pill: 6, a serving of GHB: 10.

Barcelona is a horny city. Good-looking young Spaniards, hot weather…

when summer's around, the people are practically naked to start with. And it's

a port. Random sex is nothing new to this town.

If you walk around Raval, especially along a street called San Ramon, you'll

see more hookers than front doors. Most these days seem to be from South

America or Africa – since 1978, it's not been illegal in Spain to sell your wares.

If they're not on the street, they'll be working out of 'puticlubs', the strip/live sex

joints that usually have an upstairs or series of back rooms if you're looking

for a private 'show'. The 'famosos' are reputed to hang out at one in the Sants

area called Sauna Cristal (c/Tarragona, 177; Metro: Sants,).

Whoever you're with, the traditional place for encounters of the night was, and

will continue to be, the *meublé*. The nearest translation is 'love motel', but it's

not what you think. You pay by the hour, and they're not just for the sordid and sex

the love rat. Instead, they were mostly created for couples that lived with their parents. They've existed in Barcelona for more than a hundred years and are completely above-board and legal. They're mostly very clean and contain all kinds of weird kinky extras, from mirrors to themed décor. However, after they repeatedly got involved in scandals – one time, a famous businessman was found in one with his niece – Franco ordered them all closed in 1972.

Six years later, when he passed away, they reopened immediately and most people were pleased to see them back. Everyone knows they're there and, though people still don't talk about them very much, they're a big part of the local society. If you want to spice up your relationship, there's no place like them. But enough of the history lesson. Let's have sex.

NB: the word is 'preservativos' not 'condomos'. Most chemists close at 8pm; many have 24-hour condom machines outside.

La Casita Blanca

❦

It began as café outside the city which offered rooms for the customary siesta. Instead, people began to use it for some feasting of their own.

The owners rebuilt the hotel in the city and neighbours baptised it "The Little White House" due to the never-ending white sheets sundrying on its terrace. With 50 rooms filled with opulent decorations reminiscent of the splendiferous Liceo opera house, they've thought of everything. In the early days, the concierge would even store rosaries and missals for women whose alibi was church, while recounting football game highlights and scores for the men. Generations of Barceloneans have passed through and been conceived behind its respectable doors. In short, it's an institution.

If you choose to drive – or go by cab – into La Casita Blanca, you're ushered into a private garage. Walking through the front door, however, a besuited man or elegant woman will welcome you into a discreet salon/reception area. No reservations are accepted. If the red light's on in your waiting room or bedroom, it's forbidden to enter the corridor. Chance encounters can be embarrassing or politically lethal.

An hour or two at the Casita makes you feel like a spy or an 18th-century courtly lover. The rooms are from a bygone age of dangerous liaisons, filled with heavy old furniture. They're spotlessly clean, although you can sniff a slight edge of lemon disinfectant as golden sidelamps cast a subtle glow upon the room. Drinks are passed into the room via a discrete partition. Although for me it felt more like sneaking a quickie at Granny's house than the roar of stately passion in a palace, if you get horny to Merchant Ivory, this is the place to let history carry you away.

On the corner of Av Hospital Militar & c/Ballester

Metro: Lesseps

Wander past the beckoning midget in a tuxedo, the neon extravaganza and the lurid posters announcing the venue. Pay through the nose for a drink, (it's your admission fee, so don't try to refuse) and take a seat around the stage, squeezing past drunken stag night revellers and slightly unseemly older men in weather-worn jackets. You're in Bagdad, a classic of the city's live sex scene and one of the last remaining pillars of **the glorious days** when El Raval was a genuine den of iniquity. If anyone asks, just pen your visit in as "historical research".

c/Nou de la Rambla | Metro: Parallel, Map 4 D2 | www.bagdad.com

bagdad

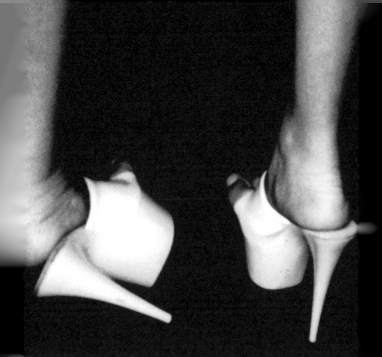

My friend took me out for a ride late one night, up the Diagonal, right into the heart of the city's learning institutes and most important businesses. He turns the wheel and we cruise slowly down the street, when suddenly a tall mysterious figure with flowing blonde hair, long legs and a raincoat materialises out of the pre-dawn light. We drive slowly past more shadowy figures ranged along the sidewalks and loitering in small groups. Tiny pieces of fabric worn as skirts, naked breasts, tottering high heels, all evoking a slight thrill wrapped around the sobriety of the posh suburban Zona Alta. And then even the pretence of a raincoat or micro-mini is shed, and suddenly the whole meaning of the area changes. **Oh my God. It's a guy.** Kind of. Well, s/he has a penis and is wearing nothing more than heels and a wig. Crowds of shemales, strolling purposefully and defiantly down the road, touting for business. Suddenly I'm a character in a David Lynch movie. Quick, let's drive round again.

c/Gregorio Marañon; Metro: Zona Universitaria

SUITE 5 CONTINENTES

When I go to make the reservation I stare at the doorbells outside a normal block of flats. I ask the porter and he points up to the first door on the right, which is labelled "Gabinete Psicotécnico". I ring the bell and the door opens with a waft of perfumed, heavy air. A woman welcomes me in, chatting away about what they do and how.

On Comte d'Urgell near c/Mallorca
Call for details on 934 546 507
Metro: Hospital Clinic,
Map 5 B2
www.suite5continentes.com

I get a tour of all 5 rooms and select the Europa. There's something about the Roman columns, cherubs and plastic grapes that just makes me shiver.

Later that night, we're ushered politely to our space with a bottle of cava in an ice bucket, a bowl of nuts and a little packet of After Eights. We run around the room. What to do first? Strip? Pop the cork? Have a smoke? Run the bath? Watch some porno? We decide to do it all, and are soon in the huge bath, up to our eyeballs in foamy water, drinks in hand, luxuriating in bubbles and steam. The piped music may not be the best (damn, should have brought a radio) and neither are the bath oils (damn, should have, etc). But the night was unforgettable. Next week: Asia. It's like travelling the world by orgasm. Did the continent move for you?

203

SEIS & NUEVE

Avenida Príncipe de Asturias, 18; Metro: Fontana; www.6y9.com
Sun-Thurs: from 7pm. Men if they select you. Women on their own,
first drink free. Fri-Sat: couples only after 10 pm. Cost: first two drinks
for two people cost €35 and then drop to €8.

This is a swinging club. What the hell am I doing here? Won't the people here be seedy, scary, letchy? But everyone who welcomes us in is amazingly friendly, explaining things, offering a tour. Apparently we've arrived late (at around 4am). But we needed a drink or five to get us here at all. Next time, they say, we should be here about midnight. Everyone's already downstairs in the "nudist zone". Great.

We stay at the bar, order drinks, watch porno. No, this is silly. Let's go downstairs and take a look. We grab some condoms and head for the stairs. If anyone fat touches me, I'll scream.

I love these big fluffy towels and little white slippers. We strip, put our clothes in the lockers and go to the lounge area. We smile politely at the young couple sitting there. The guy looks at me. He can't be undressing me with his eyes – I'm already naked. He smiles. Moans and groans ring out from all around.

I look at the jacuzzi, where at least six couples are screwing in its steamy waters. Suddenly, the guy across from us starts going down on his woman, and my man and I try hard not to stare – actually, I find it quite exciting.

We walk around to an enormous bed, at least 25 metres long with 12 couples arranged along it, in varying positions from the Kama Sutra. Ages vary but it's far from just aging couples trying to grope younger flesh. Around the corner is the "orgy zone". Seven or eight people – or maybe more, it's all just limbs and flesh – twisted together. A man puts his hand on my shoulder; it's the way of asking, are we interested? But not on our first visit. My boyfriend breathes a sigh of relief as I remove the hand (the accepted way of saying "thanks but no thanks"). The face belonging to the hand smiles, shrugs and walks away. If I'd left the hand there, I'd have agreed to a group roll. Shame, he was quite cute.

We walk back over to the huge bed. We look at each other. We look at

This is the male gay capital of the Mediterranean, with all the sexyness and Catholicism that you'd expect. Although it's much better in summertime, nightlife an sex are on offer throughout the year. But be aware: apparently seductiv gay-lookalike local kids and men may only be suburban machos pretenc ing to be fashionable. However, some of them may, depending on where and when, be available for specific contacts and experiences. For outdoo cruising lovers is the **Montjüic park**, which is fully crowded from dusk ti dawn. Anything can be found in there: cute kids, hung tops, old-schoc vouyeurs and touching approachers, plus plenty of "nor-mal" men with hidden secrets.

Flirting concentrates around the **Palau Nacional** near **Plaça Espanya**. If you want to get even closer, the classic cubicles are in the toilets of **FNAC** and especially in **El Corte Inglés** in Plaça Catalunya, or the ones at **Sants** or **Francia** stations. Down the coast, **Sitges** is practically an all-gay town, the best of the place to be found at the beach in the nudist zone of **Caldetes**. There are a couple of good beaches that are worth the one-mile walk away from town to the north. Just across the rail-road from the beach area is the cruising zone (much more crowded on weekends), an exciting green and yellow area that can seem either like a desert or a moving flesh mountain, depending on your luck that day. If you prefer some privacy back in Barcelona, try the saunas. The most visited are **Thermas** (c/Diputación, 46; Metro: Rocafort), perhaps the largest in Europe, with a selection of paid-for sex on offer; **Casanova** (c/Casanova 57, Metro: Urgell) is very well located with a younger clientele; **Corinto** (c/Pelayo 62, Metro:

Catalunya), the most central and filled with plenty of foreigners; **Condal** (c/Espolsa-Sacs, 3, Metro: Urquinaona), a classic; and **Bruch** (c/ Bruc, 65, Metro: Girona), famous for its older crowd. The bar and club scene is mainly concentrated in **Gayxample** (Metro: Universitat), stretching between c/Sepúlveda and c/Aragón, and c/Casanova and Plaça Urquinaona. **Punto BCN** (c/Muntaner, 63; bear night on Wednesdays) is the place to start the night, perhaps moving onto the cosy **G Café** (c/ Muntaner, 24) before ending up at the central focus, **Dietrich** (see following pages). It may not be easy to meet new people there but it's the place to pick up club flyers for the night. If it's Tuesday to Thursday, head for **Arena Sala Madre** (c/Balmes, 32) for the evening. A sweet pseudo-poppy place for youngsters and friends, it's much visited by gay females, and is the birthplace of upcoming local queens and stars. **Space** (Tarragona 141-7; Metro: Tarragona), on the other hand, hosts Gay Day, a fun way to end the weekend, with live performances, from 7.30pm on Sundays. If you'd rather mix music with genitalia, the hideously decadent **SM55** (Riera Sant Miquel, 55; Metro: Diagonal; quiet on weekdays) in Gracia is totally sex-oriented and themed almost every night. Upstairs you can drink, meet, look, talk. Down on the dark humid basement however, you can let yourself go as much as your desire and partners allow. There's also the recently opened **XT** (Comte Borell, 143; Metro: Urgell) a sex club that opens at 6pm till 1am, but again at 5am till 10am at the weekends for those craving a horny afters. Bears have got a few homes in Barcelona: **New Chaps** (Diagonal, 365; Metro: Diagonal) is a small bar with easygoing people; and **Bear Factory** (c/ Paseo Domingo, 3; Metro: Passeig de Gracia), open Fridays and Saturdays and only for bears and bear-lovers. Though lesbians are not so well-served by the city, the classic place is **Aire – Sala Diana** (c/Valencia, 236; Metro: Passeig de Gracia), a huge dance floor and bar visited by all kinds of girls, including lots of fashion-cloned youngsters. For something more high class, there's **Silk** at the uptown club Elephant (Ptge dels Til.lers, 1) two Sundays a month, or the bar **De Mer** (c/Platón, 13; FGC: Padua), only for those who are stylish enough to get past the doormen.

PlayaSantSebastian...

"Cerveza, Coca-Cola, Fanta, agua fria", he bellows out.
"Donuts Bambolino", goes another, *"Donuts Bambolino"*. I see at least four other vendors nearby and that's without even lifting my head from the towel. It's the time of day when the sun has become less brutal and tinges everything with a warm and golden glow – and the beach vendors go into hyperdrive. But also the time when party flyers are distributed, plans are made, wingmen are assigned, packages are checked out and ears are strained harder than the Speedos to pick up the latest gossip. There is no other time or place more essential on Barcelona's gay scene in the summer. Facing the sea, walk right – almost to the end of Barceloneta – until the male-female ratio drops like a wet noodle.

Mojama, a Andalucian friend told me, is wind-dried tuna, a delicacy from the south of Spain. It's also the word that springs to mind looking at the north side of the pool. Backgammon and card playing on the sun loungers all year round, these pensioners sport deep, leathery tans which would make George Hamilton proud. The tan line of a buff waterpolo player, suggestively peering at the top of his Speedos, brings my mind to other matters as he dives into the lap pool on the south side. Families invade the place on Sunday afternoons and the gym's packed in early evenings, but otherwise it's yours to use and peruse. Gay-friendly but suitable for anybody who needs a bit of physical activity.

Club Natacio Atletic

Pl. del Mar Sant Sebastia, Barceloneta. Three pools, full gym, direct beach access. Day pass: €8. www.cnab.org Map 1, C/D1.

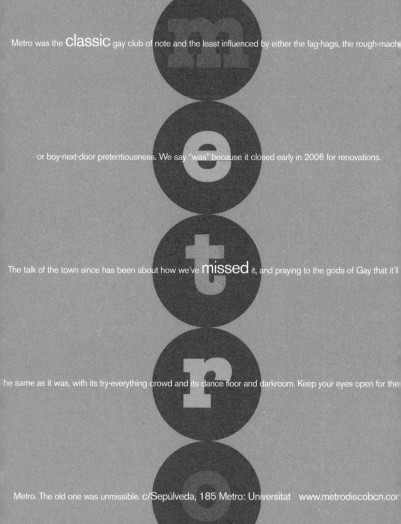

Metro was the **classic** gay club of note and the least influenced by either the fag-hags, the rough-mach

or boy-next-door pretentiousness. We say "was" because it closed early in 2006 for renovations.

The talk of the town since has been about how we've **missed** it, and praying to the gods of Gay that it'll

he same as it was, with its try-everything crowd and its dance floor and darkroom. Keep your eyes open for the

Metro. The old one was unmissible. c/Sepúlveda, 185 Metro: Universitat   www.metrodiscobcn.com

ZELTAS

C/CASANOVA 75 METRO: URGELL
WWW.ZELTAS.NET
MAP 5, C3

Zeltas attracts a more mature, fashion-oriented crowd, spiced up by smooth **Latin house** from the resident dj. Preen to be seen, but don't be intimidated – friendly **conversations** make this a great place to **Start the night in style.**

With one branch here and another in Madrid, the Eagle is the gay sex bar of choice in Spain. The entrance to the one here feels part-canteen, part-bar from which you can either head into a wooden corridor with small rooms off it, or into a short walkway with parallel rooms that are interconnected by wooden grids. It may sound complicated, but **SEX IS VERY EASY TO FIND** here: or of course you can sit, walk and talk. All kinds of sex are allowed (there's even a bath for **GOLDEN SHOWERS**), and there are regular theme parties such as **HARD SEX OR**

FISTING NIGHTS. A dress code is strictly applied ("LEATHER, RUBBER, UNIFORMS, JEANS, S+M, OR NOTHING!"), although this is regularly replaced by underwear-only (Tuesdays) or pure nakedness (Thursdays). As debauched as you would expect.

Passeig Sant Joan, 152
Metro: Verdaguer
www.eaglespain.com/barcelona

Dietrich

Elegant design — think chandeliers and velvet sofas — share space with a fine bar, acrobats, transvestite strip shows and well-dressed gay men from all over the city (and the world) in this absolute classic of the local scene. She's been here forever, and she never lost her style. If gay Barcelona were New York, Marlene would be its high-heeled, lipsticked Statue of Liberty.

Consell de Cent, 255
Metro: Universitat
Map 5, C3

There is this one spot – roughly somewhere between the coat check, the line to do a line in the ladies, and the middle handrail of the staircase – where you feel like you're attending TWO PARTIES simultaneously. To the right, three bare-chested gym bunnies are moving in synch with the bass waves of the booming house, Red Bull and water bottles in hand. To the left, a fag hag and her hag fag are gyrating wildly to this year's Spanish Eurovision winner, to which the crowd all seem to know the lyrics. Move just a little to either side and it'd be easy to forget the existence of the other.

MUSCLE marys, scene queens, leather daddies, chicken hawks, chubby chasers, closet cases, tops, bottoms – you'll find them all packed into the two very different dance floors in Salvation, the gay club of reference in town.

Fridays-Saturdays 1-6am
Ronda Sant Pere 19-21
Metro: Urquinaona
www.matineegroup.com

salvation

Sylvie at nicky boy

One wonders, just for a moment, how old this Parisian nightlife veteran really is as she struts by, Adonis boyfriend in tow. Sylvie's TDances have been a fixture for longer than she – or anyone else – cares to remember, and now they're held at Nick Havanna's, at the popular night Nicky Boy. Famed for top-notch go-go shows, great house music and eye candy to spare, it's the only thing to do after church on Sundays.

c/Roselló, 208
Map 5, B4
Metro: Diagonal
Check flyers or the website for details of parties.
ww.gaytdance.com

la bata de boatiné

In a word: indiequeer. The bar's name means "the cotton dressing gown" but don't go if all you want to do is curl up an go to sleep. Dirty, small, loud and an absolute must for people who take their queer with a twist. A temple of crazy, it's at its best on Wednesdays, Thursdays and Sundays.
c/Robadors, 18. 10pm-2.30am. Map 4, C3. Metro: Liceu

SWEET CAFE

Chic, petite and absolutely sweet, if you like your men cultured and cute, this is the place to sit at a table and sip a pre-club coffee or cocktail, while you enjoy some poppy beats, admire some queer art and show off your artistic leanings.
c/Casanova, 75; Map 5 C3
Metro: Urgell

HOTEL AXEL RELAX

Style is STYLE,
no matter what
your sexuality.
Gay-run, hetero-
friendly with its
own boutique,
and all in the
SMOOTHEST
possible taste.

c/Aribau, 33
Map 5 C3
Tel: 933 239 393
Metro: Universitat
www.hotelaxel.com

Barcelona is great.
And intense as hell.
Sometimes you have to get away.
But getting away's great too.

away from the city

Start on the fringes of the city. Montjuïc, for instance – a little mountain on the edge of the sea – hides secrets that visitors to the Miró museum always miss. On the far side is the bar Caseta de Migdia (see p.99). Nearer Plaça Espanya is a climbing wall inside a tunnel, created by an ex-policeman, called La Foixada, where a riding school also hires out ponies (take bus 50 from Gran Via and get off the stop after Poble Espanyol; go down the stairs 20m from the stop, then head left).

At the back of Barcelona is a bigger set of hills, with a large park called

Cosserola. It can be reached in no time at all by train (Ferrocarril) from Placa Catalunya. Get off at Peu del Funicular and go to the park information office for walking routes. As if the views weren't good enough, you can also walk up to the TV tower designed by Norman Foster, and take a lift to the viewing gallery (cost of renting the top floor: €1,770).

If you stay on that train a couple more stops to Baixador de Vallvidrera, you arrive at Carretera de les Aguïes, a road that snakes along the hillside, passing monied houses and pretty woods. Halfway along, you might head to Can Martí for a traditional lunch stop (see p.128). Hiding on the other side of the hills is the posh town of Sant Cugat. It's a beautiful drive and on the roadside are classic restaurants including Can Cortés (Carretera de l'Arrabassada km. 6,5, Tel. 93 674 17 04), an old-style building with great views towards the valley behind the city.

If that's not high up enough, there's always the Pyrenees. Less than three hours' drive away (buses from Estación Norte, Alsina Graells, Tel. 93 265 65 92 or from Estación de Sants, Hispano Igualadina, Tel. 900 12 35 05) are extraordinary experiences both in summer and winter. Ski/snowboarders head to Andorra or La Molina – not quite the Alps, but not bad for being in a day's reach. The posh skiing of choice for the King of Spain is the cosy village Baqueira Beret, and on the other side of the mountain from La Molina is the climbing spot Mont Grony. Dinner at the old monastery makes you feel like Heidi.

But when the sky is blue, so is the sea, and up the coast on the Costa Brava are treats such as the quiet town Sant Pol del Mar (take the FGC train from Passeig de Gracia towards Maçanet-Massanes; about a one hour ride). If you want a quicker option, Ocata, with its long wide

beaches, is on the same line.

For more lively beaches, Sitges is the place. A smaller Brighton to Barcelona's London, it's posh but laidback and a 30-minute train journey from Passeig de Gracia. For gays, it's the place to see and be seen, though chilled enough to be open to all. Spend the day at the beach and then head to Villa Lola (Paseo de la Ribiera, 2) or Restaurante Bahia next door for a cocktail, before strolling up to c/Mayor for a snack at Café Alfresco (number 33), a small and chic restaurant. At night, several bars are crammed into c/1 de mayo.

If you're driving back, Cala Morisca on the cliffs (Carretera de Garaff) is a perfect place for a quick stop – or a longer one if you coincide with one of their summer fiestas in the bay (which otherwise functions as a nudist beach). Also on the journey is Castelldefels, an unremarkable town except for Nou Lido (Passeig Marítim, 297) Beach Club and The Tropical Beach Club (c/Tallinaires, 17 – just outside in Gavà-Mar), both with private pools and beaches. Further up the coast is Cadaquez, (buses from Estación Norte, info 972 301 293, worth hiring a car as the drive is fantastic). For a simple but decent bed, try Hostal Cristina, (Riera, s/n Tel. 972 258 138) or Hostal Marina, (Riera, 3 Tel. 972 159 091). Then drive to Cap de Creuz, an old lighthouse at Spain's most easterly spot, where a small restaurant (Tel. 972 199 005) serves a mix of Spanish and Indian food. The real treasures are the rooms (around €80/night) above the restaurant. Just you, your loved one and the big blue sea.

MAP5
(EIXAMPLE)

MAP6
(GRACIA)

MAP2
(BORN)

MAP4
(RAVAL)

MAP3
(GOTHIC)

HOW THE **MAPS** FIT

MAP1
(BARCELONETA)

BARRIOS

BARCELONETA - MAP 1

WEIRD
Kiss of death, 40
RELAX
Rompeolas, 94 C4
Biblioteca de les Aigues, 96
EATING
Jaica, 115 A2
Central Catalana de Pollastre, 128
Vaso de Oro, 114 A2
Torre de alta mar, 118 C1
Can Majó, 140 C2
DRINKING
Kasbah, 168 A2
CDLC, 179 C5
Shoko, 179 C5
NIGHTS OUT
Catwalk Club, 179 C5

BORN - MAP 2

Introduction, 136
SLEEPING
Banys Orientals, 19 B2
Five Rooms, 28 B2
Gothic Point, 17 A2
WEIRD
La Cuna de Oro, 38 A2
SHOPPING
Vinoteca, 52
Walking tour, 66
Lobby, 78 C5
Mercado del Born, 172 B4
RELAX
Estacio de França, 95
EATING
La Panadeta, 115
Casa Casals, 43 C1
Princesa 23, 108 A3

L'economic, 108
Bar Mundial, 109
Euskal Centre Cultural, 109 B3
Textil Cafe, 117 B3
Espai Sucre, 118 A5
La Bascula, 124 B4
Agullers, 127 C2
Itzli, 130 B2
La Habana Vieja, 138 B3
Pebre Blau, 138 B3
Santa Maria, 141 C5
Pizza del Born, 130 C4
DRINKING
Casa Paco, 43
Kiriki, 157 B3
Espai Rai, 165
La Fianna, 168 B3

GOTHIC - MAP 3

Introduction, 127
SLEEPING
Center House, 16 B2
Residencia Victoria, 12
Neri, 22 C2
WEIRD
Frederic Mares Museum, 39 C2
SHOPPING
Glove and hat shops, 60
Walking tour, 62
So_da 141, D2
New Concept Store, 65 B2
Comité, 65 B2
Music shops, 72 E2
Heritage, 75 C2
Dom, 78 D2
Leoni, 103 B1
RELAX
La Granja, 92 C1
Cafe Estiu, 101 C2

MAP2

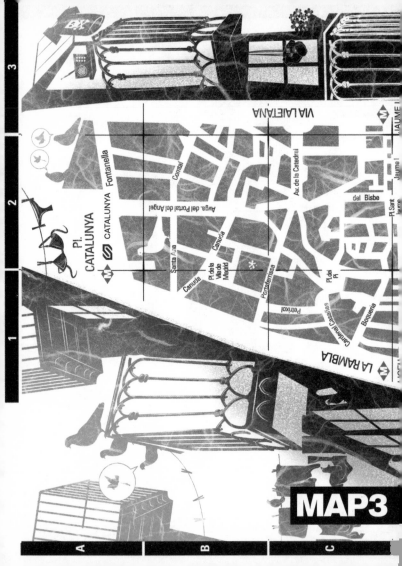

MAP3

MAP4

EIXAMPLE

uda Diagonal

Enrique Granados

Rosselló

PROVENÇA

DIAGONAL
Ⓜ

rca

Balmes

Rambla de Catalunya

Passeig de Gràcia

Pau Claris

Ⓜ
PG. GRÀCIA

talanes

Ⓜ
Pl.
versitat

Ⓢ
Ⓜ
Pl.
Catalunya

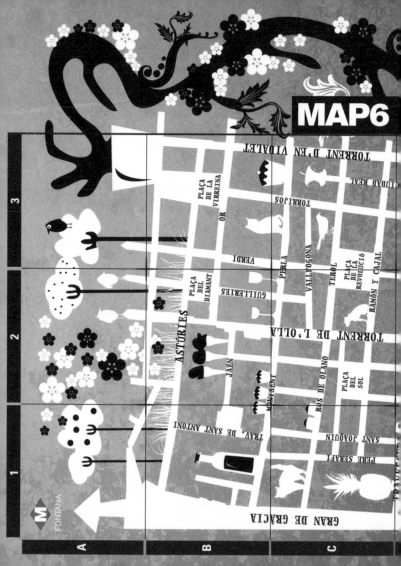

MAP6

IF MOBY CAME TO BARCELONA HE MIGHT THINK THAT the view of the vertical garden outside his Casa Camper hotel room (Elisabets, 11, Tel. 933 426 280) leaves him hungry for some green. The best way to start the day may be some meditation in the Botanic Garden (Parc de Montjuïc), with its calm aesthetics and soothing views. Then he would head back into town for lunch at Organic (Junta de Comerc, 1) with a cup of tea and chat at the Hari Krishna Temple (Placa Real, 12). He would finish off the afternoon with an extended session at Anahata Yoga (Aribau, 61) before meeting up with friends at Hivernacle (Parc de la Ciutadella) – a compromise between style and plantlife – for dinner.

LET'S SAY DESIGN GURU MARC NEWSON IS PASSING BY FOR A VISIT. HE MIGHT start the day early, looking for odd discarded objects at the Encants Vells fleamarket (Glories). When hunger can no longer be ignored, he heads over to Palo Alto (Pellaires, 30-38), the design studio of local guru Mariscal, and has lunch in the open air in the canteen. On the way back to the centre of town, he drops in at Freaks (Ali Bei, 10) for the latest in Spanish graphic novels, goes by Foto Casanova (Pelai, 18) to admire the collection of old Leicas, and then Ras (Doctor Dou, 10) for all he can consume of design books and magazines. He ends the afternoon at Modulolab (Book ahead, tel. 659 978 977), scouting for strange lamps and funky furniture. With all of that sent ahead to his hotel, he makes it to modernist classic Pavelló Mies Van de Rohe (Marquès de Comillas, 7) just before it closes for the day. As the evening sneaks up, he goes for early drinks at Dry Martini (Aribau, 162) and then dinner at Flash Flash (La Granada de Penedes, 25) before it's time to return to Hotel Omm (Roselló, 265).

JAMES DEAN HAS BEEN REBORN AGAIN AS A CATALAN AND IS LOOKING FOR A MAD NIGHT OUT so he has a quick shot of pastis in Bar Pastis (Santa Mónica, 4), moves up to Marsella (Sant Pau, 65) for an absinthe – no sugar – and then hangs out in c/Robadors, watching other people start trouble, smiling to himself. He greets some of his favourite prostitutes, laughs off their remarks, and sneaks away towards Bagdad (Nou de la Rambla, 103), giving the midget doorman a few smokes on the way in. He flirts with the girls backstage, shakes his head at the embarrassing stag parties out front, and when the place finally kicks him out, he hitches a ride to afters bar Bang Bang (Gran Vía 580). That's the last thing he remembers before waking up, a girl asleep at his side wearing only his leather jacket, in the middle of the maze (Laberint d'Horta, Passeig Castanyers, 1).

JUST ARRIVING IN HIS OWN HELICOPTER IS **DONALD**. "I want to go there," Mr Trump says, "and there, and there too." waving his hand in the air. The view from the Hotel La Florida (Crta. Vallvidrera, 83-93, Tel 932 593 000) isn't so bad, even for a billionaire with his own Manhattan tower. A limo ride down the hill takes him to Mantequeria Ravell (Aragó, 313) for brunch – their foie and poached egg a snip at €100 plus. A brief meeting in the executive room at the top of Torre Agbar (Placa de les Glories), and business is done for the trip. To butter him up, his hosts rush him over to Quimet & Quimet (Poeta Cabanyes, 25), where he mixes with the locals, and impresses them by ordering their dustiest, priciest bottles with nary a blink. A short snooze, then the O2Wellness center (Eduardo Conde, 2-6) strips him of more sweat than money, and as his hair is drying, he barks "Take me to the best seafood in the city," and a quiet table at Botafumeiro (Gran de Gràcia 81) is his for the evening.

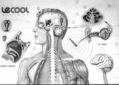

WHAT IS LE COOL?

It's a weekly magazine. It's a book.
It's going to be huge. It changes your life.

We began in 2003 with a free weekly e-magazine in Barcelona. le cool magazine is a funky agenda and a guide to the city's cultural life, a highly selective 'what's on', a good friend who's always in the know. It soon spread to Madrid. Now we're in Lisbon, Amsterdam and London too, with Berlin and Milan soon to follow.

We're passionate about cities and what's in them. As well as cultural events, we also recommend bars, restaurants and unusual experiences, always with an eye for the personal and unpredictable. We interview local personalities and showcase local designers. We publish in local languages, and have teams of contributors in each city.

Rather than only searching for the latest or the hippest, we just look for things that are worth your time. We never, ever accept payment or favours in return for content.

We publish le cool magazine weekly, arriving in your inbox to help you make the most of where you live. Visit www.lecool.com to check it out.

We also do other things. This is our first book. It won't be our last.

Do you know where we're going next?
Tell us: idea@lecool.com

CREATED BY
LE COOL PUBLISHING

FOUNDER/CONCEPT
RENÉ LÖNNGREN

EDITORIAL DIRECTOR
ANDREW LOSOWSKY

WRITING
Andrew Losowsky
Alex Brahim (p.206-7, 210-216)
Ana Cristina Canizares (p.131-4)
Casey Butterfield (p.35, 45-8, 95)
Eva Thomás Mora (p.49-63, 66-7, 70-1)
Filipa Gramos (p.82-3)
Gabriela Holland (p.16-7, 28, 84-5, 185)
Joana Pinto Correia (p.192-4)
Jon Anderson (p.72, 174-6)
Llibert Figueres (p.103)
Mary T. Bauer (p.195-205)
Maite Felices (p.76)
Mia Rappoport (p.58, 66-7, 68, 74-5)
Michael Fuchs (p.53, 128, 208-9, 214)
Rafa Gimenéz (p.72, 174-6)
René Lönngren
Susy Taylor (p.53-5, 62-3, 70-1, 104-5)

EDITORIAL ASSISTANTS: GABRIELA HOLLAND,
RIGO PEX

DESIGN FERICHE BLACK
CREATIVE DIRECTOR: RICARDO FERICHE
ART DIRECTOR: ROCÍO HIDALGO
DESIGNERS: IVÁN CASTRO, OSCAR ARAGÓN
MICHELE TENAGLIA
ASSOCIATE DESIGNER: ÁNGELA MARÍA MARÍN

PHOTOS
Andrew Losowsky
Dany Vives (p.132-4)
Diana Kandic (p.71)
Ivan Castro (p.30, 36, 49-51, 86, 110, 126, 174-6)
Jack Ristol (p.72, 180-84)

Jordi Sarrá and Ricardo Feriche (p.204-5)
Judith Luna (p.33, 162)
Lisbeth Salas (p.38, 79, 104, 111, 120, 122-3, 129, 161, 171, 201, 208)
Maite Felices (p.77)
Mariano Herrera (p.63, 118, 135-9)
Maxi Holland (p.16-7, 28-9)
Nicolas Neufcourt (p.24, 53-63, 66-71, 74-77, 159, 166, 171)
Oriol Terrats (p.149)
René Lönngren
Ricardo Feriche (p.32)
Rocío Hidalgo and Ricardo Feriche (p.11-3, 195-7)
Sandra Myhrberg (p.35, 64, 90, 94, 102, 168)
Takuro Takeuchi (p.100, 177, 218-221)

ILLUSTRATIONS
Boris Hoppek (p.186-7)
Carmen Segovia (p.6, 246)
Juliet Pomés Leiz (p.60-1, 95, 199)
Sarah Stothart (p.142, 192-4)

MAPS
Vasava Artworks, www.vasava.es

—————————————

THANKS TO
Ana Portolés, Sebas Taberna, Annaloes van Gaalen, Isabel Lindim, Rafa Gimenéz, Gonzalo Samaranch, Charlotte Lemaitre, Raquel Gariani, Gaute Hovdal, Enric Ysamat, Neil, Llibert Figueres, Nacho Rapallo, Pichi & Blanca, Ricardo Gadea, Wawas, Charly, Isaac at Montana, Marc Ros, Manuel Garriga, Joakim Borgström, Sonia Bermejo Simon, Michaele Tabucchi, Reinaldo Rojas, Ana Mas, Enrique the secret police-man, Javi Risco, Alex the Large, RollsRoger, Joana Pinto Correia, Jordi Vilches, Práxedes Garcia Molina, Vasava Artworks, Pepo Montsant, Georgios Diamantis, PlushPeople, My Favourite Things, Rob Shreeve, Paul and Clare and everyone at Friday Books.

PRINCIPAL TYPEFACES: Akzidenz Grotesk BT, Galliard BT, Giza, Eldorado
CALLIGRAPHY: Iván Castro

—————————————

Did you like it? Loathe it? Did we miss something?
Let us know: idea@lecool.com **www.lecool.com/book**

Leftov

Five photos guaranteed to make friends not in Barcelona jealous: hot bodies at the beach, the view from Tibidabo, drinking in one of the beachside chiringuito bars in April/October, the graffiti in the streets behind the Boqueria market, something blurred at 4am taken in the flat of some funky, good-looking people you just met.

Ana (editor of le cool magazine Barcelona) is an avid fan of odd bars and the punky side of things, so the best way for her to spend 22h-03h any day of the week would be starting at bar/restaurant Babia (c/Sagristans), with some great tapas and wine. Then it's off for drinks at Mercaders (c/Mercaders), where rock-fanatic owner Ramon will greet guests saying "Bon día" (good morning) from midnight on. Last stop before heading to Sala Apolo (c/Nou de la Rambla), a cocktail at La Penultima (c/Riera Alta 40), where the kitschy entrance reveals all you need to know about the crowd.

The best way to find addresses on the map is to visit http://www.bcn.es/guia/welcomea.htm

To find out about the clubbing scene try record stores Tasmaniac, Ramallers, 15 for dance/rave recommendations or CD Drome, Valdoncella, 3, for indie tips. For rainbow recommendations try Ovlas, Via Laietana, 33, where staff are well informed and well equipped. Good places for flyers during the day: RAS (c/Doctor Dou), the shopping centre with the camel on c/Porteferissa.

Ricardo, creative director extraordinaire of this book, suggests the best visual experience of Barcelona begins in the harbour at

Port Vell, going up c/Carabassa. Next, you should search out Plaça Sant Felip Neri near the cathedral, which is a beautiful place to sit in the Spring. Finally, cross the city and get lost in the park with the labyrinth in Horta.

You can drink the water, but it doesn't taste nice. Bottled is very cheap in supermarkets – but better still...

...mixing cheap red wine with cheap, clear fizzy lemonade (la Casera) is a great summer thirst-quencher. Any bar will serve it – just ask for a tinto de verano.

Andrew, the editorial director of le cool, loves having breakfast with a good book at the outside tables of Kasparo (Plaça Vincenç Matorell). If it's brunch time, he always orders the focaccia. In the evenings, a quiet beer in El Nus (c/Mirallers) suits him just fine.

On Sunday, the only shops open after lunch are Opencor (various places around the city, open till after midnight, seven days a week) or those owned by people of Chinese or Pakistani origin. Try Raval. The only exception to that rule is Maremagnum, the shopping centre in the main port near the bottom of the Ramblas, open all day for normal shopping needs.

If you only have time to do one thing while in Barcelona, René, le cool's passionate founder, says you should head for Tibidado, Barcelona's mountain backdrop, and go for a ride in the Ferris Wheel, located just to the right of the church which can be seen from all over the city – the most spectacular view you could ever imagine.

ers

Places not to fly to by mistake: Barcelona, capital of Anzoátegui State, Venezuela; Barcelona, Sorsogon province, Phillipines; Barcellona Pozzo di Gotto, Sicily. But if you do, send us a postcard.

Still want to know more? Let le cool show you around in person. Email concierge@lecool.com

ISBN 1-905548-22-2

Written and edited by le cool publishing
Published by Friday Books
www.lecool.com
ISBN 1-905548-22-2
978-1-905548-22-4
Come find us. We're on the map.